RELIABLE
ELECT

Other titles in the Sailmate series

How to Paint Your Boat
Nigel Clegg
ISBN 0 7136 4097 9

This book answers all the DIY boatowner's questions, explaining in non-technical terms correct surface preparation, dealing with defects, correct application methods and giving advice on storage times and estimating quantities.

How to Design a Boat 2nd edition
John Teale
ISBN 0 7136 4914 3

A very practical book to enable even first-time designers to produce a worthwhile boat design. John Teale takes the reader step by step through the stages of designing both power and sailing boats, whilst also explaining the reasons behind the process.

How to Choose the Right Yacht
Joachim F Muhs
ISBN 0 7136 3950 4

This book shows how interested buyers can assess all the qualities of a boat from the comfort of home!

How to Use Radar
H G Strepp
ISBN 0 7136 3324 7

Radar technology is explained, including how different types of sets work, how they should be operated and the use of radar for navigation and collision avoidance.

How to Cope with Storms
D V Haeften
ISBN 0 7136 4109 6

Sailors need to be able to recognise well in advance the approach of a deep low pressure system, to prepare for safe navigation during the passage of a storm, and then be able to handle the boat safely whilst it rages. This book, packed with practical advice and information, will help readers cope with all these aspects.

How to Trim Sails
Peter Schweer
ISBN 0 7136 3323 9

This practical best-selling guide covers tuning the rig for varying conditions for masthead, swept-spreader, fractional, fractional with running backstays, and dinghy rigs.

SAILMATE

RELIABLE MARINE ELECTRICS

How to upgrade your system

 Chris Laming

ADLARD COLES NAUTICAL
London

Published 1999 by Adlard Coles Nautical
an imprint of A & C Black (Publishers) Ltd
35 Bedford Row, London WC1R 4JH

First edition 1999

ISBN 0-7136-49194

A CIP catalogue record for this book is available from the British
Library.

Typeset in Century Schoolbook by
Rowland Phototypesetting Ltd, Bury St Edmunds, Suffolk
Printed and bound in Great Britain by
J W Arrowsmith Ltd, Bristol

Contents

Introduction   ix

1 Batteries: energy reservoirs   1

2 Choosing batteries   5
What size do I need?   5
Types of battery   5
    Lead acid batteries   5
    Gel batteries   9
    Nickel cadmium batteries   10
Water tank comparison   13
    Lead acid battery–water analogy   13
    Gel battery–water analogy   13
    Nickel cadmium battery–water analogy   13

3 Battery connections and wiring   16
Battery terminals   16
    Solder type battery connections   16
    Threaded stud terminals   16
    Screw terminals   17
    Clamp connections   18
Protecting against corrosion   18
Bus bars and connection blocks   19
Battery wiring   20

4 Charging   22
Charging methods   22
    Taper (or resistance) charging   22
    Three-stage charging   25
    Constant current charging   26
    Pulse charging   26
Charging equipment   27

Alternators   27
  Alternator controllers   28
  Three-stage regulators   29
  Heart Interface incharge regulator   30
  Constant current regulators   30
  Pulse current regulators   31
Mains-powered battery chargers   32
Solar panels   36
  Wind-powered generators   37
  Water-powered generators   37

5 Distribution   40
Isolating switches   40
  Rotary switches   40
  Key switches   41
  Choosing and installing isolating switches   41
Fuses and circuit breakers   42
  Engine starting circuits   43
Panels   43
Cable and wiring   45
Conduit, trunking and support   45
  Cable trays   46
  Trunking   46
  Slotted trunking   46
  Conduit   48
  Tie bases and 'P' clips   48
  Connections   50
  Soldering   50
  Crimping   50
Deck fittings   51

6 Monitoring   52
Voltmeter   52
Ammeter   52
Amp-hour meter   54

7 On board equipment   57
  Lighting   57
    Energy efficient lighting   57
    Halogen lights   58
    General lighting   58
    Night lights   58
  Refrigeration   59
    Water-cooled refrigerators   59
    Holding plate refrigerators   59
    Evaporator refrigerators   59
    Insulation   61
  Using the engine to power equipment   61
    Autopilots and instruments   62
    Instrument power consumption   63

8 Case histories   64
  Case history 1: *Flint*   64
  Case history 2: *Rival Spirit*   66
  Case history 3: *Stray Cat*   67

Glossary of terms   73

Appendix 1 Amp hour consumption table   75

Appendix 2 Cable size table   76

Appendix 3 Equipment manufacturers' addresses   78

Index   83

Acknowledgements

I would particularly like to thank the owners of the three yachts featured in the case histories that make up Chapter 8 of this book: Rob – *Flint*, Chris and Liz – *Rival Spirit*, and Geoff and Gillian – *Stray Cat*.

While I was writing this book Geoff and Gillian were on a world cruise. They had settled in Portugal for a while when Geoff died suddenly, well before his time. So much of this book is based on the work I did on *Stray Cat* that I can only regret he will not see its publication.

My thanks also to all the manufacturers of the products mentioned, and to their staff, for the help they provided.

Introduction

Whether you are setting out on a round the world voyage or on a week's holiday, ensuring that your boat's electrical system is reliable is one of the best investments you can make for peace of mind and a comfortable life on board.

A system which is energy-efficient will not only increase safety and reduce electrical consumption, but will probably be more reliable, because its lower power consumption reduces the risk of any of its components being overloaded.

As a boat owner you are responsible for generating your own power. Once you appreciate this, and realize how limited your generating capacity is compared with a household supply, wasting energy by leaving lights on will become a thing of the past.

This book is intended to give the cruising yachtsman or motor cruiser owner an insight into how the electrical system on board can be made as reliable and efficient as possible.

At the heart of the electrical system are the batteries. Not everyone has an understanding of batteries and their function, so I have introduced a water analogy of batteries in Chapter 1. This compares a battery with a water tank, on the assumption that everyone understands how water is stored in a tank and how it is subsequently used. The same analogy is used in later chapters, to illustrate other aspects of marine electrics, such as charging and distribution.

The types of batteries installed on a boat are important, because they must match the use to which they are being put. Chapter 2 deals with the advantages and disadvantages of the various types available, to help you decide which type is most appropriate for your boat and budget.

Even after you have chosen the right batteries, they will not be of much use if the connections to them or the cables from them are unsuitable. Different connections, terminals and cables all have their own pros and cons, which are covered in Chapter 3. They are also the first part of the complete distribution system, made up of the isolating switches, circuit breakers, and wiring that are dealt with in Chapter 5.

Whichever types of batteries are installed, they will need charging. Here too, there are various options that range from engine-driven alternators and mains-powered battery chargers to non fossil fuel methods such as solar panels and wind- or water-powered generators. The idea is to recharge the batteries in the minimum time and with the minimum effort, so Chapter 4 is devoted to the characteristics of these different charging systems.

Ideally, the complete electrical system should be monitored, so that you know how it is performing and whether any faults are developing. This is covered in Chapter 6.

Energy efficient equipment reduces the demands made on the batteries, and minimizes the time the engine may need to be run just to keep them charged. Chapter 7 shows that even something as apparently insignificant as the correct choice of lighting will reduce the electrical consumption, while the power expended on refrigeration – often one of the largest consumers of electricity on board – can be cut dramatically by choosing a water-cooled unit.

Finally, I've rounded off the book by looking at three case histories which illustrate, in a practical way, how the contents of the earlier chapters can be applied.

1 Batteries: energy reservoirs

Batteries provide a reservoir of energy on board any vessel that uses electrical power.

It may sound strange to suggest that the electrical characteristics of a battery can be compared to a tank of water, but I think this is one of the best ways to understand electrics at work, because it is easy to visualize the energy stored in the battery as being like water stored in the tank. In this sense, a battery that is 100% charged is equivalent to a full tank, while a 50% charged battery is equivalent to a tank that is half full, and a battery that is flat is like an empty tank (see Figs 1.1 and 1.2).

Water tank	Battery
Water level in tank	Charge level in battery
Volume of water (cubic litres)	Charge (amp hours)
Flow of water out	Current flow
Resistance to flow	Circuit resistance
100% full	100% charge
80% full	80% charge
50% full	50% charge
0% full (empty)	0% charge (flat)
Water pump	Charging device
Filling pipe	Charging circuit
Water meter	Amp hour meter
Flow monitor/shut-off valve	Circuit breaker
Valve	Switch

An isolating switch allows the power stored in the battery to be released in a controlled fashion, just as a valve controls the flow of water from the tank, while the wires and circuit breakers that distribute the power are analogous to the pipes and valves that distribute water from the tank.

We could ascertain the water level in the tank by monitoring the rate at which water is flowing out and comparing it with the rate at which it is being pumped back in. The same is true for the level of charge in the battery, which can be assessed by monitoring the

1

charge used (in amp hours) and the charge replaced by the alternator and/or other charging devices.

If the water flow through a pipe is too high, perhaps because the pipe has burst, a flow monitor detects this and operates a shut-off valve to shut off the supply and stop the leak. Similarly, if the current flow in a battery circuit is too high, a fuse or circuit breaker is used to isolate the supply to stop the circuit being overloaded (See Fig 1.3).

Just as the water level falls when water is taken from the tank, so as charge is used from the battery its charge level falls. If this process were to continue, eventually the tank would empty and the battery would be left without any charge, or 'flat'.

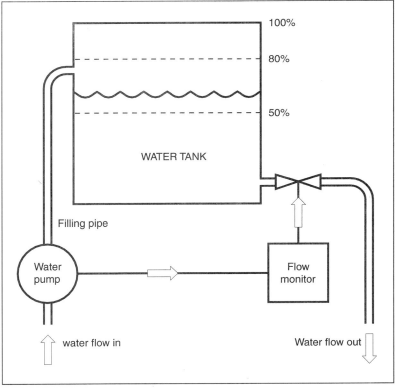

Fig 1.1 Principle features of a water tank.

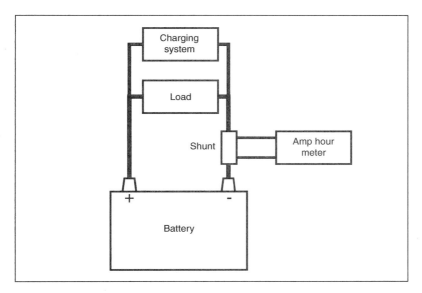

Fig 1.2 The principal features of a battery circuit.

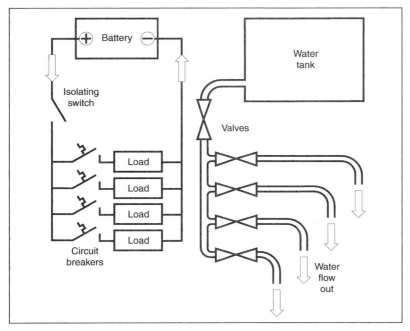

Fig 1.3 Circuits connected to a battery are equivalent to output pipes from the water tank.

Ideally, as water is used from the tank it is also being replaced, so as to maintain the maximum level. Likewise, as charge is used from the battery it too should be replaced. The electrical equivalent of the water pump is an alternator or some other charging device.

Switching additional parallel loads into the output circuit of the battery is like opening valves to additional outlet pipes from the tank, ie the overall flow out increases. The parallel loads result in a decrease in resistance of the overall circuits connected to the battery. The lower the electrical resistance of the circuits, the higher the current flow out of the battery (see Fig 1.3).

2 Choosing batteries

What size do I need?

The size of battery bank required will depend on how many amp hours you expect to use over a period of, say, 24 hours, and the type of battery used. (See Appendix 1 for Amp Hour Consumption table.)

The amp hours required will be based on the estimated consumption, in amps, of all the equipment to be used in the 24 hour period. For example, if the average consumption is 5 amps then the overall amp hours will be 5 amps × 24 hours = 120 amp hours.

This does not mean that a 120 amp hour battery will be enough: we need to allow an extra safety factor, depending on the type of battery employed. For a lead acid battery, a safety factor of 2 is used, for gel batteries the safety factor is 1.3 and for nickel cadmium batteries the safety factor is 1.

Size of battery required will be:

120 × 2.0 = 240 amp hours for lead acid
120 × 1.3 = 156 amp hours for gel
120 × 1.0 = 120 amp hours for nickel cadmium

Types of battery

There are three types of battery in reasonably common use on boats:

- Lead acid
- Gel
- Nickel cadmium

Lead acid batteries

Lead acid batteries are available in various types and capacities. The main types are engine start (heavy duty), semi-traction, traction, low maintenance, and maintenance free.

Engine start batteries are designed to produce a high current for a limited period, so they are made from thin plates, mounted close together in the electrolyte so that there is a large effective surface area and the current has to travel only short distances.

When used for their intended purpose of starting engines, they are likely to discharge by about 10%, but this loss of charge will be replaced almost immediately by the engine's alternator. These batteries are not designed for deep cycle applications such as providing domestic power for a cruising yacht.

Many boat owners fit large commercial vehicle batteries in the belief that a larger battery will be better able to provide power for their boats' domestic services. In reality, though, these batteries are just larger versions of small engine start batteries, so they are no better at withstanding the effects of deep cycling.

Maintenance of engine start batteries is done by removing their cell covers and adding distilled water as necessary.

Semi-traction or **leisure batteries** have thicker plates than engine start batteries, allowing the current to be released more slowly but over a greater period of time.

This means they can be used for applications such as the tail lifts on trucks, and for the motors of electric wheelchairs and golf trolleys, but as they are also capable of producing the short burst of power required for engine starting they are well-suited for use in caravans, motorhomes and boats.

They are generally slightly larger and more expensive than engine start batteries and can usually be maintained by removing their cell covers and topping up with water as necessary.

Traction batteries are the type used on fork lift trucks. They are designed for very heavy deep cycle use, so they are not suitable for regular use for engine starting. In any case, they require charging at higher voltages than can usually be achieved by an alternator and are available only as individual 6 volt or 2 volt cells. Building a bank of cells to create a battery of the required voltage results in more expense, weight and size.

Low maintenance batteries usually have provision for topping up with distilled water, although their design is such that they can recombine the gases of hydrogen and oxygen created during charging back into water. The recombination is only about 95% effective, so a small amount of water will be lost in the event of gassing and topping up will be required. A release vent prevents excessive build up of pressure in the event of overcharging or the charge voltage being too high.

Maintenance free batteries are usually sealed, so topping is impossible. Although it is almost inevitable that a battery will lose some of its electrolyte over a period of time, the makers of maintenance free batteries overcome this by overfilling them during manufacture.

Batteries with **lead calcium** plates produce virtually no gases during normal operation so they do not lose electrolyte to the same extent as normal **lead antimony** plated batteries. They also have lower self-discharge rates (Fig 2.1).

Disregarding traction batteries, the advantages and disadvantages of lead acid batteries are given below.

Advantages of lead acid batteries

- Relatively cheap
- Readily available throughout the world, and widely understood
- Lighter than equivalent gel or nickel cadmium batteries
- Maintenance free versions are available
- Some have charge indicators
- Lead calcium versions have improved self-discharge characteristics compared with lead antimony plate construction

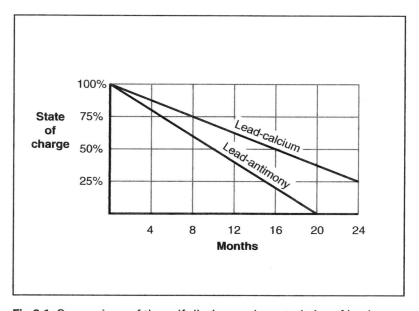

Fig 2.1 Comparison of the self-discharge characteristics of lead antimony and lead calcium plated batteries.

Disadvantages of lead acid batteries

- Maximum life span limited to about four to five years
- Deep discharges (below 50%) cause internal damage, and repeated deep discharging has a cumulative effect that can significantly reduce battery life
- Life span decreases with rise in temperature
- Toxic and explosive gases are produced
- The electrolyte is acidic and highly corrosive
- Self-discharge rate is higher than other types, so should be fully charged when stored and require regular recharging when stored for long periods
- Require a safety factor of 2 to be applied when calculating battery capacity requirements:
  ie capacity required = estimated consumption × 2

Delco Voyager lead calcium plated batteries.

Gel batteries

The construction of gel batteries is similar to lead acid batteries except that the electrolyte is gelled instead of liquid. The nature of the electrolyte is such that it does not spill out of the battery even if it is inverted or damaged, and the battery, being fully sealed, is completely maintenance free. Each cell is sealed, so although it has its own pressure relief safety valve, any gases produced during normal charging are recombined and returned to the cell.

Gel batteries are well suited to deep cycling, so they are particularly appropriate as domestic service batteries, and their self-discharge rate is so low that a fully-charged gel battery should retain 50% of its charge even after two years in storage, without the need for recharging.

One drawback of gel batteries is that charging has to be performed correctly and at a controlled rate, otherwise they are prone to damage by overheating. The reason for this is that in any battery, heat is generated within the electrolyte near the plates while it is being charged. In a conventional lead acid battery the liquid electrolyte is free to move, so the warm electrolyte near the plates can rise, helping to dissipate the heat. In a gel battery the electrolyte is more solid so it cannot distribute the heat so quickly. It is rather like the difference between heating a pan of water and a can of beans: you can boil the water quickly without stirring because the water can move itself, but you have to heat the beans very slowly or else stir them to make sure the ones at the bottom don't burn.

Advantages of gel batteries

- Totally maintenance free
- No leakage of electrolyte if the case splits
- Can be inverted without spillage
- Can be deep discharged
- Low self-discharge: can be stored for up to two years and maintain more than 50% charge without the need for recharging
- Classed as non hazardous for transport purposes
- Long life, up to ten years
- Lighter per amp hour than nickel cadmium batteries
- Cheaper than nickel cadmium batteries

Gel batteries from Sonnenschein.

Disadvantages of gel batteries

- Overcharging can cause excessive build up of gas in the battery
- More expensive than equivalent lead acid batteries
- Heavier than equivalent lead acid batteries
- Not so good for regular use as engine starting batteries
- Require a safety factor of 1.3 to be applied when calculating battery capacity requirements:
  ie capacity required = estimated consumption × 1.3

Nickel cadmium batteries

In the past, nickel cadmium batteries (sometimes known as 'ni-cad' or 'alkaline' batteries) have always needed high-voltage charging systems that made them impractical for most marine applications. That, however, is changing, and some of the latest types can be charged by almost any conventional charging system.

This is the case with nickel cadmium batteries. Instead of using pocket plate construction, which requires charge voltage up to 1.7 volts per 1.2 volt cell, the construction of nickel cadmium cells with sintered positive electrodes and plastic bonded negative electrodes

(SRM batteries from Saft Nife) allows a charging voltage of 1.45 volts per cell, or 14.5 volts for a ten cell bank in a 12 volt system. The charging method can be constant current, constant voltage, taper or pulse allowing virtually any charging system available to the marine market to be used.

Nickel cadmium batteries can tolerate a variety of abuses that would damage more conventional batteries, including overcharging, voltage reversal, deep discharge and complete discharge.

They require virtually no maintenance and can be expected to last 20 years or more, so although their initial cost is higher than any of the other types, they may work out cheaper in the long run.

Serious blue water cruisers, in particular, should think about using nickel cadmium batteries to ensure a reliable electrical system without having to worry about trying to replace their batteries in some far-flung corner of the world.

Advantages of ni-cad batteries

- 20 years or more life span
- Can be overcharged without damage
- Can tolerate voltage reversal without damage
- Can be completely discharged without damage (to 1 volt per cell)
- Can be stored discharged for two years
- Topping up required only every two to ten years depending on type and use
- Operating temperature range of −20°C to +70°C
- Can withstand 2000 complete charge/discharge cycles
- Resale value of vessel is increased
- Terminal voltage remains higher on discharge, so current flow is less than with lead acid or gel batteries in similar situation
- Electrolyte is potassium hydroxide and therefore is not corrosive if spilt, unlike electrolyte in lead acid batteries
- Gases are not toxic
- Battery amp hours required = calculated amp hours × 1

Disadvantages of ni-cad batteries

- Expensive
- Gases are explosive
- Heavier than equivalent lead acid or gel batteries
- Slightly larger space required, but single cells can be arranged to suit the space available, whereas lead acid and gel batteries are of fixed dimensions.

Nickel cadmium batteries from Saft Nife as fitted into *Stray Cat* (See case history 3). The bank on the left is an 80 amp hour battery for engine starting. The bank on the right is a 220 amp hour battery for domestic power.

Price and usable amp hour comparison

Service battery	Type	Approx price (1998)	Usable service amp hours
400 amp hours	ni-cad	£2500 (US$4250)	400
400 amp hours	gel	£1100 (US$1870)	307
400 amp hours	lead acid	£500 (US$850)	200

Water tank comparison

Recalling the water analogy, the three types of batteries can be illustrated by different types of water tanks (See Fig 2.2.).

Lead acid battery–water analogy

A lead acid battery can be compared with a steel water tank, that can be expected to last only four to five years before rusting through.

Its outlet pipe is half-way up the tank, so its useful capacity is only about 50% of the total. (In reality, lead acid batteries can be discharged to lower levels than this, but only at the risk of reducing their life span even further.) To make up for this, the total volume of the tank has to be doubled to achieve the effective capacity required.

The self-discharge rate of lead acid batteries is higher than that of the other types. This can be equated to leakage from the tank: in this case the leak is more serious than that of the others, so if the tank is left for a period of time without being refilled it will gradually empty. In the case of a lead acid battery, self-discharge means that the battery cannot be left for long periods without being recharged.

Gel battery–water analogy

A gel battery is equivalent to a galvanized steel tank, with an expected usable life of ten years. Its height is greater than its width, giving a greater flow of water at lower water levels and corresponding to a battery that can be discharged to a lower level and still produce a useful output.

This tank, however, has only a small vent, so if it is filled too quickly there will be a build up of pressure inside. This could damage the tank, in the same way as rapid charging damages gel batteries.

Nickel cadmium battery–water analogy

A nickel cadmium battery is akin to a tank made of stainless steel, which should remain serviceable for 20 years or more.

It can withstand overfilling without damage and is greater in height than in width so that it can give useful output at low levels and maintain a good flow even when nearly empty, just as nickel cadmium batteries can be overcharged without damage and can be

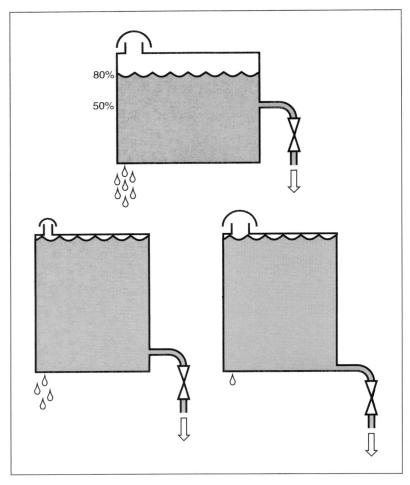

Fig 2.2 Different types of battery can be compared to different types of water tank: here, a typical lead acid battery (top) is compared with a gel battery (bottom left) and a nickel cadmium battery (bottom right).

discharged to zero charge (not zero volts) without damage. (Zero change is when the cell voltage is 1 volt per cell or 10 volts for a 10 cell 12 volt bank.)

This tank hardly leaks at all, just as the self-discharge rates of nickel cadmium batteries are very low.

3 Battery connections and wiring

There is no point in having a fully charged battery if the connections to it are so poor that the electrical energy being drawn from it falls at the first hurdle.

Returning to the water analogy, resistance to the flow of current in a wire can be equated to resistance to the flow of water in a pipe, such as might be caused by deposits of limescale in a hot water system.

If the connections to the water tank are loose, corroded or blocked they will leak, so the pressure in the pipework will fall. Likewise if the connections to the battery are loose, corroded or dirty, then they will introduce resistance to the flow of current and this, in turn, will introduce a voltage drop into the circuit.

Battery terminals

Three types of clamp terminal may be used to make connections to the round tapered posts of standard batteries.

Solder type battery connections

Making a soldered battery connection involves heating the entire joint to a temperature high enough to melt the solder. Unfortunately, in practice, it is quite likely that the outer strands of the cable will be soldered, but not the inner strands. If a soldered joint subsequently fails at sea, the chances of achieving a satisfactory repair are slim.

If repairs are required, they should be done away from the batteries to avoid the risk of igniting battery gases.

I do not recommend soldered joints on battery terminals.

Threaded stud terminals

Threaded stud battery terminals require the cable ends to be terminated with crimp lugs (cable end terminations fitted over the cable strands and compressed or crimped onto the strands to obtain the required connection) which fit over the stud and are secured by

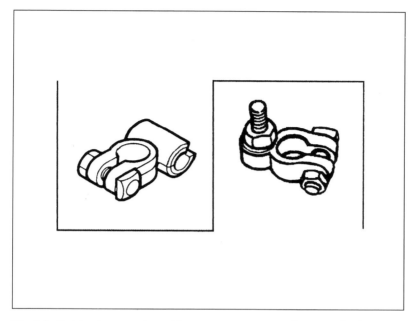

Fig 3.1 Solder type and stud battery post connection terminal.

nuts and washers. This type of terminal makes it particularly tempting to connect several cables to one stud, making the terminal look like a spider. If any cable has to be removed, or another added, some of the other cables may have to be removed as well.

Recommendations by the American Boat and Yacht Council (ABYC) and International Standards are for a maximum of four connections per stud terminal.

I do not recommend the use of 'butterfly' nuts for securing the terminals on the studs, because finger tight is not good enough and if you use pliers or a spanner to tighten them there is a risk that you will break their wings off. In any case, if you are going to have to use tools, then you may as well use a normal nut, which will make a tighter connection.

Screw terminals

No cable terminals are required for this type of connection: the strands of the cable are simply fed into the tunnel of the terminal and clamped in place by screws. Unfortunately this can damage the strands, but the effects can be minimized by withdrawing the

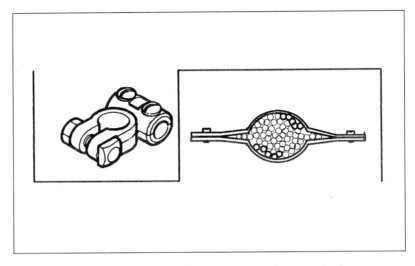

Fig 3.2 Screw type and clamp battery connection terminal.

screws and filing their ends to a rounded shape before assembling the connection.

If repairs are required, this is probably the quickest and easiest type to deal with, because all that is required is to cut back the insulation from the wire before remaking the connection.

Clamp connections

Terminals with clamp connections do not always provide a tight connection throughout the cable strands, because some strands tend to be squeezed out of the clamp as it is tightened.

If this method is used, the strands should be twisted as tightly as possible, to overcome the tendency to spread as the clamp tightens onto the strands.

Protecting against corrosion

Any connections on or near the batteries may be subject to corrosion caused by the battery gases. To guard against this, it is normal practice to apply an anticorrosion compound or petroleum jelly to the terminals.

It is important, though, to keep the mating surfaces of the joint (ie the battery posts and the inside surfaces of the clamps) clear of anticorrosive compound.

These areas should be kept dry and clean, avoiding any form of contamination which may insulate the contact surfaces, increasing the electrical resistance of the connection, the voltage drop and the heating effect.

The heating effect of an electric current is $I^2 \times R$, where I is the current (in amps) and R the resistance it is passing through (in ohms).

If, for instance, a connection imposed a resistance of one ohm and 20 amps were being drawn through it, the heat generated would be $20 \times 20 \times 1 = 400$ watts.

Imagine the effect when drawing a starter motor current of 200 amps through the same joint ($40,000 \times 1$ watts). Normal resistance of a joint would be a matter of milliohms, so the heating effect is not so dramatic.

Bus bars and connection blocks

Ideally, the number of connections made direct to a battery should be kept to a minimum, partly because multiple connections tend to be untidy and unreliable, and partly because if any repairs or modifications have to be carried out at sea it may be impossible to add or remove one cable without disturbing the others. Not only will this disrupt the power supply to some services, but it may also cause sparks.

It is much better to use one large cable, capable of carrying the maximum expected current flow, from the battery terminal to the isolating switch. From the load side of the switch two connections can be made, one to the starter motor and one to a connection block or bus bar to feed other circuits, such as distribution panel, bow thruster, anchor windlass etc if fitted.

For maintained supplies, ie bilge pumps, intruder alarms etc, that require continuous connection to the battery, it is important to connect fuses or circuit breakers as near to the battery as possible for these circuits, but outside any battery box or compartment to eliminate the risk of igniting any gases.

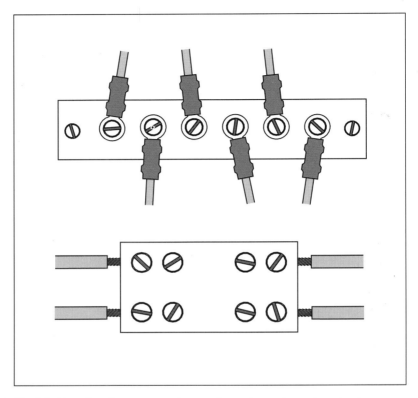

Fig 3.3 Top: bus bar connections using crimped eye terminals secured by screws. Bottom: connection block using screws to grip the wire strands.

Battery wiring

Battery wiring needs to be flexible and large enough to cope with the current that may be drawn through it.

Some cables are available with tinned strands to enhance corrosion resistance. These cables are recommended by the ABYC for use in the marine environment, even though they impose slightly more resistance than non-tinned cables.

Whichever type is used, cable suppliers should be consulted for resistance values – usually given in ohms per kilometre or ohms per 1000 feet – if voltage drop calculations need to be made.

In the UK and Europe the most popular battery cables are

tri-rated cable, welding cable and auto wiring cable, all of which are multistranded and flexible.

Tri-rated cable is PVC insulated at a rating of 105°C.

Auto wiring cable is also PVC insulated but with a lower temperature rating of 70°C.

Welding cable is sheathed in a very flexible polyethylene compound with a temperature rating of 85°C and also has tinned conductor strands.

The temperature ratings given above are for the conductor temperature, which is a combination of ambient temperature and temperature rise of the conductor due to current flowing in it.

Similar cables (marine grade) are available in the USA, mainly with tinned conductor strands to meet the highest specifications of the ABYC.

I would recommend a minimum cable size of 35 mm² (2 AWG) for engine battery wiring and starting circuits. As it is standard practice to use the service batteries for emergency engine starting it makes sense to use the same size of cable for the service batteries as the engine batteries.

AWG	Metric equivalent (mm²)	Metric cable size (mm²)
20	0.52	0.75
18	0.82	1.00
16	1.32	1.5
14	2.1	2.5
12	3.3	4
10	5.32	6
8	8.5	10
6	13.5	15
4	21.3	25
2	33.7	35
1/0 (0)	53	70 (50 if current capacity not exceeded)
2/0 (00)	67.6	70
3/0 (000)	84.4	95
4/0 (0000)	107	120

Fig 3.4 Conversion table: American wire gauge and metric cable sizes.

4 Charging

Although we tend to think of a battery as 'supplying' electrical power, it is really only a storage device. Power that is taken out of it has to be replaced or else, sooner or later, the battery will go 'flat' and we will be left without power.

Charging methods

In Chapter 1, the process of charging a battery was compared to filling a water tank, with the water pump being described as the equivalent of an alternator, battery charger or other charging device.

The characteristics of alternators and most cheap battery chargers are such that they can only achieve about 80% charge because of the internal resistance of the battery. It is rather like a water pump that can only pump water up to a certain height.

In the case of lead acid batteries, which cannot be discharged below 50% of their charge without the risk of internal damage, this means that only about 30% of a battery's nominal capacity is actually available.

To overcome this, the 'pump' needs to be improved if it is to pump water to a greater height, and the alternator or battery charger's performance needs to be improved to overcome the internal resistance of the battery and achieve something approaching 100% charge.

Various methods can be used, of which the three most popular are:

- Three-stage charging
- Constant current charging
- Pulse charging

Taper (or resistance) charging

Taper (or resistance) charging is the term used to describe the way ordinary engine-driven alternators supply power to a battery. The fact that they can only achieve about 80% charge is not a problem

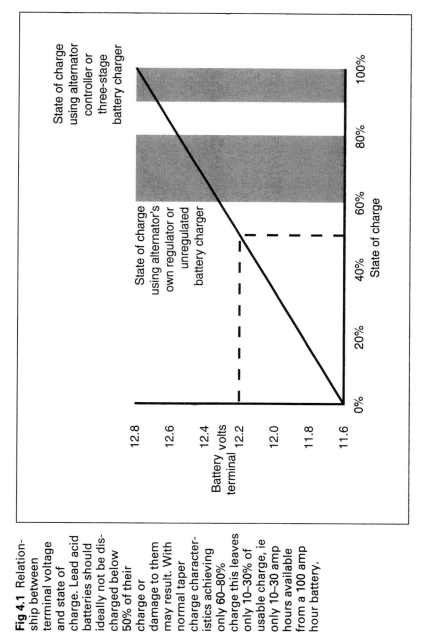

Fig 4.1 Relationship between terminal voltage and state of charge. Lead acid batteries should ideally not be discharged below 50% of their charge or damage to them may result. With normal taper charge characteristics achieving only 60–80% charge this leaves only 10–30% of usable charge, ie only 10–30 amp hours available from a 100 amp hour battery.

in the automobile industry, because it is quite enough to replace the charge taken out of the battery during engine starting, and to provide for normal loads such as lights etc while the engine is running.

An alternator is normally regulated so that its ouput voltage never exceeds a pre-set level – usually between 14.0 and 14.4 volts. When the battery charge is low, its voltage is also low, so the relatively high voltage from the alternator can easily overcome the opposing voltage of the battery, and can therefore pump charge into the battery quickly.

Once the charging process is under way, however, chemical changes inside a battery mean that its internal resistance increases, opposing the flow of electricity.

Then as the battery becomes more fully charged, its voltage increases and offers even more resistance to the electricity flowing from the alternator.

To overcome this, a second stage of charging is required – which is where three-stage charging comes in.

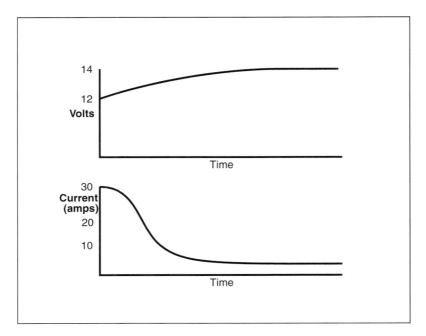

Fig 4.2 Taper charging: as the terminal voltage rises, the output current from the charger decreases.

Three-stage charging

Three-stage charging has become more popular as electronic technology has advanced, because it can ensure that batteries are 100% charged quickly and without damaging them.

The three stages are:

- The **boost** or **bulk** charge stage
- The **equalize** charge stage
- The **float** or **maintenance** charge stage

During the boost or bulk charge stage, the output current from the charger is kept at its maximum until the battery terminal voltage reaches a preset level – normally 14.25 volts for a 12 volt system. Once this level has been reached, the battery is 80% charged.

The next stage – the equalize charge – maintains the voltage at the finishing voltage of the boost charge, and gradually decreases the current over a set period of time to a trickle charge. At the end of this stage the batteries are 100% charged. If charging were continued at this voltage, the batteries would start to gas so the charger automatically moves on to the next stage.

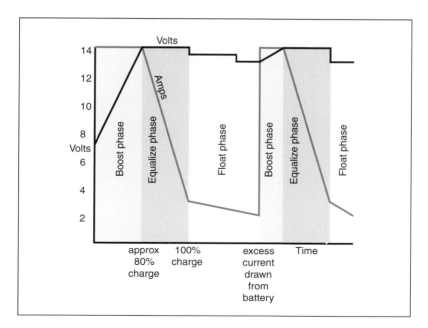

Fig 4.3 Three-stage charge graph.

During the float or maintenance charge stage, the charging voltage is reduced to 13.5 volts. This is below the voltage at which a battery is likely to gas, but reduces the current flow to a trickle. If a large load were to be applied to the batteries that would cause the terminal voltage to drop significantly, the charger would then revert back to the boost charge and the cycle continues.

Constant current charging

Constant current charging is another method of charging similar to the boost phase of three-stage charging. When the voltage across the battery terminals has reached its preset value, the controller senses it, switches off and the alternator reverts back to its own regulator. This method achieves a higher rate of charge because of the higher voltage used and effectively converts the alternator into a two-stage charger. The high charge rate will produce some gassing in lead acid batteries so only those with provision for adding water should be used. This method of charging is not recommended for gel batteries but is suitable for nickel cadmium.

Pulse charging

Pulse charging is where the voltage is pulsed, ie raised and lowered, for set periods of time designed to put as much charge into the batteries without causing excess gassing. Periods at which the volt-

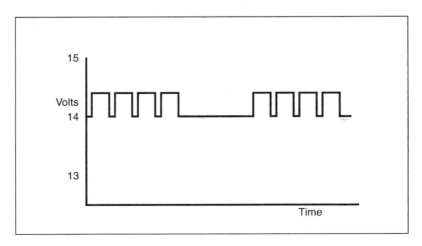

Fig 4.4 Pulse charging cycle.

age is at the low level allow the battery to rest before the pulse charging cycle continues (see Fig 4.4). Pulse charging is suitable for all types of battery.

Charging equipment

There are various types of equipment that can be used to charge a battery:

- Engine-driven alternators
- Mains-powered battery chargers
- Solar panels
- Wind-powered generators
- Water-powered generators

Alternators

The taper charge characteristics of a standard alternator can be a drawback on a cruising yacht, where the maximum charge is required in the shortest time.

An engine-driven alternator is often described as 'machine sensed' because it is regulated by sensing its own output. On an automobile, this arrangement is fine, because the alternator will be charging just one battery through a relatively short run of cable.

On a yacht, however, the output from the alternator may well be routed through a split charge diode or relay, a changeover switch or battery isolating switches, any of which introduces longer cable runs and more connections into the charging circuit and risks increasing the voltage drop between the alternator and battery.

To overcome this, the alternator's regulator can be set up so that it monitors the battery terminal voltage. This allows it to compensate for voltage drops in the charging circuit by raising its output voltage.

The conversion process involves connecting a wire from the alternator's sensing circuit, through a fuse, to the battery terminal, but a more common method of achieving a similar result is to install an alternator controller or booster.

Alternator controllers

There are several types of alternator controllers available. Although all of them are fitted outside the alternator itself, some are designed to be used with the existing regulator while others replace it completely, and some are adjustable while others are not.

My personal preference is to use a controller that works in conjunction with the alternator's existing regulator, and that can be switched on and off manually. That way, if a fault develops in the controller, it can be switched off and the alternator allowed to go on using its own regulator, providing a fail-safe system.

The addition of an alternator controller means that the alternator is likely to be producing more output than usual, so it is likely to get hotter. This means it is essential to make sure it receives plenty of cooling air to prevent overheating, especially in an enclosed engine compartment and in tropical climates.

There are a variety of regulators available. The three main types are **three-stage charging**, **constant current charging**, and **pulse charging**.

A big advantage of alternator controllers is that they can offer more sophisticated charging patterns than the straightforward taper charging available from a standard alternator.

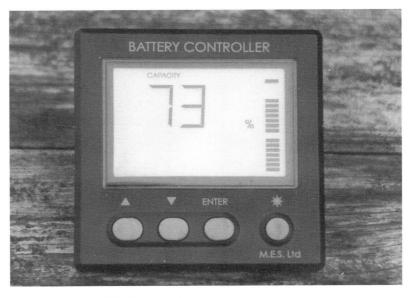

The MES control/display head.

Three-stage regulators

These regulators feature the boost, equalize, float (or bulk, acceptance, float as known in the USA) method of charging.

The two units described here – from MES Ltd and Heart Interface – can be adjusted, so they are compatible with lead acid and gel batteries. Both these regulators can replace the alternator's existing regulator. Consult the manufacturers or their agents for suitability for charging nickel cadmium batteries.

The MES battery management system, for instance, combines a battery monitor with a three-stage charge controller that can be adjusted to suit the various lead acid or gel batteries.

The MES regulator is mounted separately from the alternator, leaving the alternator's own regulator in place but can, if necessary, override it by connections made to it. This is dependent on the characteristics of the alternator regulator and the MES instructions for the type of alternator fitted should be followed. The MES regulator is designed to operate with negatively controlled alternators. These are the most common type used in Europe but positive controlled regulators are used by Motorola and some other manufacturers in the USA.

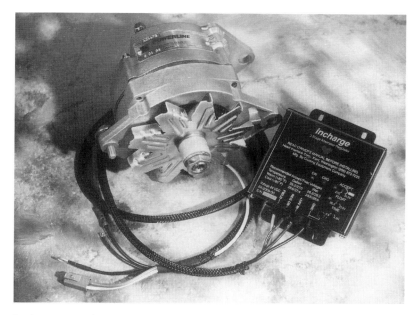

Incharge regulator.

Heart Interface incharge regulator

The incharge regulator unit has adjustment for bulk charge voltage and float charge voltage of the three-stage charging system it uses. It can also be adjusted for the time it is in the equalize (absorption) charge stage as well. LEDs indicate that the unit is on and charging and also the state of charge. It replaces the alternator's own regulator and is mounted separately but near the alternator.

Constant current regulators

The Kestrel alternator controller is a constant current regulator used in conjunction with the alternator's own regulator.

It works by allowing the output voltage of the alternator to increase until it reaches a preset cut off value which can be adjusted but which is factory set at 15.2 volts. Once this voltage is reached the controller switches off and allows the alternator's own regulator to resume control.

The current output can also be adjusted – Kestrel recommend setting it at two-thirds to three-quarters of the alternator's rated maximum – and it can be fitted with a switch to allow it to be manually controlled if required.

Kestrel alternator controller.

The high cut-off voltage required to overcome the internal resistance of a conventional lead acid battery means that I would not recommend using a Kestrel to charge gel batteries, though it would be fine for ni-cads.

Pulse current regulators

The Adverc battery management unit is a pulse charging regulator that can be used in conjunction with the alternator's own regulator and can be fitted with a switch to allow the alternator to revert to normal operation if required.

Its cycling programme normally involves 5 minutes at 14.0 volts followed by 15 minutes at 14.4 volts, but after four of these cycles there is a 'rest' period of up to 40 minutes at 14 volts, depending on the state of charge of the battery, while the voltages can be adjusted to suit different types of battery.

A temperature sensor is fitted in the connection to the positive battery terminal and the charging voltages will automatically compensate for ambient temperature variations around the batteries.

The Adverc battery management unit.

Mains-powered battery chargers

There are three main types of mains-powered battery chargers available.

Automotive types are relatively cheap, but are usually unregulated, so they should not be left charging a battery for long periods as they may damage the battery by overcharging it.

The other common variety, the 'trickle charger', is also relatively cheap but has a finishing voltage in the order of 13.5–13.8 volts, and is similar in performance to a standard alternator so it cannot charge a battery to full capacity.

The third type is more expensive, but offers the advantage of three-stage charging, to fully charge the batteries quickly.

When choosing a battery charger, its output should be rated at 20% of the battery's rated capacity – this is the optimum charging current – ie for a 100 amp hour battery, a charging current of 20 amps is recommended. A charger with a higher output may be used, as three-stage chargers will not overcharge the battery: the only disadvantage is that it will cost more!

Most of the better models can be adjusted to suit the type of battery used, so if you are using gel or ni-cad batteries, the charger supplier should be able to make any necessary adjustments to the charger.

Battery performance is reduced as its temperature rises. In particular, performance figures are given at ambient temperatures of 20–25°C. If ambient temperature and charging are high the internal temperature of the battery will be high. In a lead acid battery performance will be reduced and water lost through evaporation. (For the effect of temperature on gel batteries see page 9.) Ni-cads can tolerate higher temperatures although some water may be lost through evaporation.

Temperature compensation can be added to some modern chargers to reduce the rate of charge as the battery temperature increases, which is an advantage in tropical climates.

To illustrate what is currently available, details of Victron and Heart three-stage chargers are given below.

The Victron Energie Titan chargers are solid state and based on high frequency switching technology making them up to 80% smaller and lighter than comparable transformer based chargers. The three-stage charging process is incorporated into the design, as is a stabilized output voltage which allows it to be used as a power supply in applications without batteries.

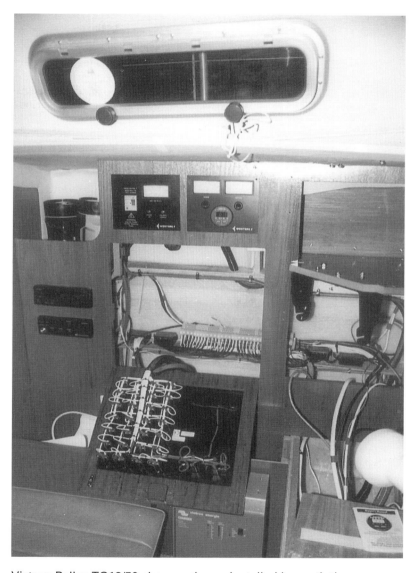

Victron Pallas TG12/50 charger shown installed beneath the
control panel. Note the row of rail-mounted terminals connecting
the panel wiring to the boat wiring (see page 43). Also note the
monitoring panel (top right) with voltmeters for engine and
service batteries and the link 10 battery monitor. See overleaf
for the completed installation.

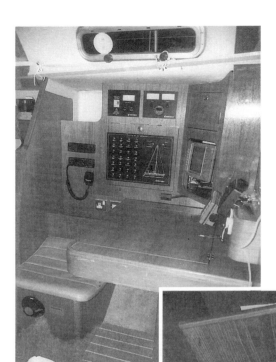

The completed control panel (above), previously seen on page 33. This navigation area is a good example of neat and efficient use of space on board. The seat for the chart table (below) doubles as a secure box for service batteries.

Adjustments can be made to the charging parameters to enable all types of battery to be charged. A voltage sense circuit detects the battery terminal voltage and adjusts the output to compensate for any volt drops in the charging circuit. Temperature compensation is provided by means of a sensor. A separate output is available for charging the engine start battery independently of the main output. If the mains supply to the unit is limited, an optional remote control panel limits the charging current output and therefore the load on the mains supply.

The Heart Interface Freedom charger/inverter is a transformer-based unit that acts as a DC to AC inverter as well as an AC to DC battery charger. It incorporates three-stage charging plus a manually initiated equalizing charge for occasional use, every few months or so, to condition the batteries. A higher voltage, 16.3 volts, is applied for a limited period to clean sulphate from the battery plates (lead acid) and bring all cells up to the same potential.

When shore supply is initially connected, and the charger goes into high output mode, its current demand from the shore supply, when used with other AC appliances, may cause the shore supply circuit breaker to trip.

Heart Interface Freedom charger.

The Freedom's charger operation incorporates a 'power sharing' capability where it automatically reduces the input current to the charger when other AC appliances are drawing from the AC supply, thereby ensuring continuity of supply and reducing nuisance tripping.

Solar panels

Solar panels consist of a number of cells manufactured from silicon in such a way that they produce electricity when visible light is incident on them. By connecting the cells together in series the desired voltage output is achieved.

Solar panels provide an ideal method of charging batteries that works even in temperate climates because it is ultra violet light – present in ordinary daylight, not just in direct sunlight – which is converted into electricity. A modern 55 watt panel can achieve an average of about 20 amp hours per day, though of course this depends on the weather, the angle at which the panel is inclined to the sun, and so on (see Case History 2).

The location of the panels, however, is important. Decks are obvious locations but the risk of damage to the panels is high. Pilot house roofs or solid cockpit spray hoods are better, especially as the curvature of the roof will improve the angle of the panel to the sun. (See Case Histories 1 and 3). Flexible panels can be fitted to canvas spray hoods and removed when necessary.

The efficiency of solar panels can fall as their temperature rises, so rigid panels need to be mounted with an air gap underneath to help them stay cool – a precaution not required for flexible panels, which have stainless steel backing plates to conduct heat away.

It is also important to make sure that the panels are kept clean, as dirt or salt on the panel will reduce the amount of light reaching the cells.

Regulators for solar panels often have a separate output that can be used for circuits independent of the battery isolating switches such as bilge pumps, intruder alarms and courtesy deck lights.

Wind-powered generators

Wind-powered generators harness the power of the wind by using a fan or turbine to drive a generator, so they have to be mounted out of harm's way to prevent the risk of crew being injured by the spinning rotor.

In general, the larger the output required, the larger the size of rotor that will be needed and the higher the wind speed has to be before the generator will start working, so when choosing a wind generator, important points to look out for are the cut in speed and its rating.

The cut in speed is usually round 6 or 7 knots on most units, but the output ratings quoted by the manufacturers are usually the maximum output available and can only be achieved at wind speeds above 30 knots. It is a good idea, therefore, to look for the output quoted at more typical wind speeds, in the range between 10 to 20 knots.

Check that the price includes a regulator – it usually does – as well as any 'dump resistors' required to dissipate excess energy as heat when the batteries are well charged.

It pays to shop around, but do not be swayed entirely by price, because some of the more expensive units offer higher outputs at lower wind speeds.

Water-powered generators

Water-powered generators are usually driven by towing an impeller/turbine unit behind the boat, rather like a trailing log. This converts some of the energy, that would otherwise be used to propel the boat, into electrical energy.

The minimum effective towing speed is generally about 2 knots, but it is also important to check the drag that will be imposed. This is usually expressed as a weight, typically 10–20 kg (22–44 lb) as a load on the towing line which will vary with speed through water.

When the generator is first deployed, the tow rope inevitably begins to twist before the generator shaft starts to rotate, but in practice this is not a problem: if anything, it helps because the twisted rope acts as a shock absorber to protect the generator from undue stress. Once the rope is twisted, every revolution of the turbine induces a corresponding revolution of the generator shaft.

Reliable Marine Electrics

Aquair water-powered generator from Ampair UK.

When cruising, a generator such as the Aquair will provide continuous charging, producing about 80 amp hours over 24 hours at a towing speed of 5 knots.

Summary of charging over 24 hour period		
Solar panels	2 × 55 watt	40 amp hour (10 hrs daylight)
Wind generator	100 watt	72 amp hour (15 knot wind)
Water generator	100 watt	80 amp hour (at 5 knots)

5 Distribution

It is the job of the distribution system to carry power from the battery (or batteries) to the various pieces of equipment that use it, as safely, reliably, and efficiently as possible.

Battery isolating switches and fuses/circuit breakers provide protection for wiring and equipment. Secure connections throughout the electrical system will ensure minimum volt drop and reduce overheating at the joints with possible fire risk.

Returning to the water analogy, electrical connections that are loose are like pipe joints that are loose. A loose pipe joint will cause a leak which will reduce the pressure in the pipe. Loose or corroded electrical connections introduce resistance into the circuit and, as a consequence, volt drop. Burst pipes are like a short in the electrical circuit. Automatic shut-off valves, which operate to shut the pipe if the flow exceeds the valve's rating, are the equivalent of circuit breakers or fuses which break the electrical circuit should the current flow exceed their rating.

Isolating switches

Isolating switches, as the name suggests, are used to isolate the batteries from the rest of the electrical system. Not only does this make it possible to work on the system without having to physically disconnect the battery; it also reduces the risk of the battery being accidentally discharged by equipment being left switched on or by minor faults in the system. Perhaps most important of all, an isolator switch virtually eliminates the possibility of an unnoticed defect causing sparks or heat that could set fire to the boat when it is left unattended. The two most common types of isolator switch are rotary and key.

Rotary switches

Rotary isolator switches are mainly intended for systems with two banks of batteries, as they are designed to allow either bank or both banks to be connected at once, simply by turning the selector knob. Rotary isolator switches are also available as on-off switches.

40

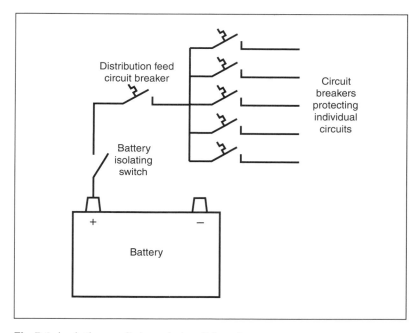

Fig 5.1 Isolating switch and circuit breakers.

Key switches

Key type switches provide simple 'on or off' connection to a single battery bank – so if you have two banks of batteries, you need at least two isolator switches. In practice, it is a good idea to have a third isolator switch to couple the two banks together for emergency engine starting.

Choosing and installing isolating switches

Whichever type of isolating switch you choose, it is essential that it is built to take the heaviest current that is ever likely to pass through it. To help you select the right one, isolator switches are usually marked with two ratings: 'intermittent' and 'continuous'.

An isolator with a 'continuous' rating of 300 amps, for instance, may have an 'intermittent' rating of 450 amps.

It is usually the 'intermittent' rating that will determine your choice, as it must be sufficient to carry the very high current drawn by the engine starter motor and the intermittent rating should be for five minutes and not seconds. Some cheap models from the Far East may have an intermittent rating of 175 amps to 200 amps – not high enough for starting many engines.

Rotary switches manufactured in the USA usually have the highest ratings and are relatively inexpensive whichever side of the Atlantic you may reside. See Figure 5.1 for circuits incorporating isolating switches.

When mounting an isolator switch, it is important to make sure that you have good access to the stud terminals to which the cables are to be connected, bearing in mind that the space behind the switch is often restricted. Also the length of stud will determine the number of connections that can be made, often only two per stud.

With rotary switches in particular, it is popular to mount the switch over a large hole in the boat's panelling, with the cables routed in from behind to gain better access to the terminals. This often results in loops of cable to enable the cable to be connected to the terminal and may require the lug, crimped to the end of the cable, to be bent so that the lug will mate squarely with the terminal stud. The alternative method is to route the cables through the panelling and then up to the switch terminals. Although the cables are visible, it makes it easier to lay the cables neatly and securely.

A third option, if you can get good access to the back of the panelling, is to cut a hole large enough to take the circular body of the switch, and to mount the switch from behind the hole, leaving the back of the switch completely accessible.

Fuses and circuit breakers

As the electrical distribution system splits into the various branches that supply individual pieces of equipment, each circuit should be protected by its own circuit breaker or fuse. These act as a kind of electrical safety valve, or as weak links, to shut off the power supply to a circuit if the current flow increases to a dangerously high level.

To do this, it is important to make sure that the rating of the fuse or circuit breaker is no higher than the rating of the cable in the circuit it is protecting. With fuses, in particular, there is a temptation to replace a blown fuse with one of whatever rating happens to be available, or even to deliberately fit a higher-rated fuse in place of one that regularly blows. In either case, the circuit is left without adequate protection. To avoid this, you may need to carry a wide selection of spare fuses.

My preference is to use circuit breakers. Although they are more expensive in the first instance, they offer better discrimination in protecting wiring, they operate more quickly than fuses, and can be reset instead of replaced when they 'blow'. Of course, the fault that caused the breaker to trip has to be rectified before it can be reset. It is also a good idea to have one or two spare circuit breakers on board, just in case it is the breaker itself that fails.

Engine starting circuits

There is, however, one major exception to the principle of protecting each individual circuit, and that is the engine's starter motor. Although there is a school of thought that says this should be protected by a high-rated fuse or breaker, I believe that it is better to be especially careful to protect the starter motor cables from damage or abrasion, rather than risk the possibility of the fuse or breaker blowing and leaving you unable to start the engine at what may be the most critical moment.

Panels

The panel which carries your circuit breakers (or switches and fuses) should offer easy access to both front and rear, with each switch or breaker clearly labelled with its function. The label should also correspond to the label shown in the boat's wiring diagrams: there is plenty of scope for confusion if the breaker labelled 'Inst 1' on the wiring diagram is labelled 'Radar' on the front of the panel and 'Aux 2' on the back!

LEDs to indicate which circuits are switched on are a useful addition, and fault indication LEDs to indicate the failure of navigation lights etc provide an added safety factor.

The photos on page 44 are 'before' and 'after' photographs showing the improvements that can be made to a boat's distribution panel. In this case, the size of the panel is limited by its location, but the top photo shows how matters were made even worse by the way the wiring had been connected to the breakers, making it impossible to open the panel without pulling some of the connections off.

Stray Cat's panel before her refit.

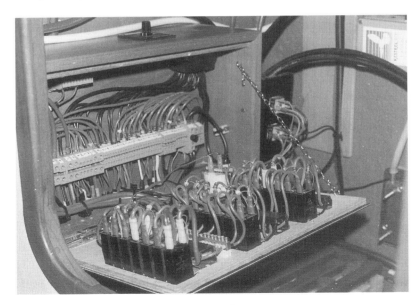

Stray Cat's new panel.

In the bottom photo, you can see that although there are the same number of breakers:

- The panel can be opened without pulling wires off the breakers.
- An individual power supply to each breaker ensures minimum voltage drop.
- The output from each breaker is taken to the row of rail-mounted terminals with the positive and negative terminals for each circuit alongside each other.
- The output wire from each circuit breaker is labelled with a number that corresponds to the number at the other end of the wire, which corresponds with the number on the terminal to which it is connected.

If panels are to be hinged they should, ideally, be hinged at their lower edge. This keeps the panel stable when opened at sea and enables anyone who needs to work on it to do so without the panel swinging to and fro.

Cable and wiring

When looking at your wiring, check for the following points:

- The size of wire must be adequate for the current it is to carry.
- The size of wire must also be adequate to keep the voltage drop to within acceptable limits, particularly in the case of long runs such as those to masthead lights.
- Wiring that leaves cable runs in tray/trunking should be adequately sleeved to protect against chafe.
- Wiring with natural rubber sheathing should be replaced with flame retardant cable as it is flammable and deteriorates with age and temperature.

Conduit, trunking and support

Electrical connections are intended to allow a flow of electricity, not to support the physical weight of the wire attached to them, or to cope with the movement of a wire swinging as the boat pitches and rolls. Similarly, electrical cables are intended to carry current rather than to withstand the continuous bending and stretching that can cause strands to break through metal fatigue. It is important, therefore, to ensure that cables and connections are adequately supported.

There are several possible methods, but in general terms any kind of support made of PVC is suitable because it is fire retardant and electrically insulating. As the main cable runs are usually out of sight behind fixtures and fittings, the aesthetics of the support is not that important.

Cable trays

Cable trays provide a support to which cables can be secured by means of plastic cable ties. This makes it easy to add extra wiring and is useful for securing cable that has to run vertically. When all the wiring is mounted in parallel it looks neat and professional and makes locating and tracing of particular wires much easier. Although galvanised steel cable tray is readily available, PVC has many advantages; it is flexible, does not corrode, is electrically insulating, is easily cut to required lengths, does not leave sharp edges when cut and drains well when wet, ie from condensation.

Trunking

Trunking is usually square or rectangular in cross-section, with a clip-on lid that hides the wiring from view, so it is cosmetically neater than cable trays.

On the other hand, it has a number of drawbacks. For one thing, the wires inside lay loose so they can often become tangled, while in vertical runs the entire weight of wire is supported by a corner at the top of the run. In horizontal runs, there is a strong possibility that the wires will all fall out if the lid is removed, and that if any oil, water or vapour is present it will stay trapped inside the trunking for a long time. Trunking lids, once they have been removed, are often very difficult to get back in place. Slotted trunking is ideal for use on the rear of circuit breaker panels or to feed wiring to terminal rows.

Slotted trunking

Slotted trunking is similar in some respects to ordinary trunking, except that it is less rigid and less cosmetically attractive, but it overcomes some of the drawbacks. In particular, it allows water, oil

A sprawling mess of wires (above) is neatly secured to a plastic cable tray (below)

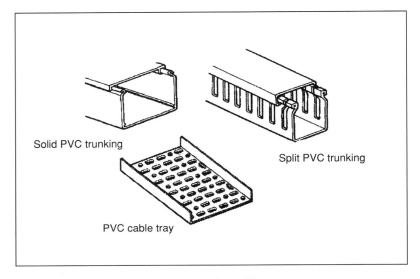

Solid PVC trunking

Split PVC trunking

PVC cable tray

Fig 5.4 Examples of cable trays and trunking.

or vapour to drain away more quickly, and allows easier access to the wiring.

Conduit

Conduit is very much like trunking, except that it does not have removable lids, and is usually supplied in a choice of round or oval cross-sections. As with trunking, wires lay loose inside, and may be surrounded by trapped water, oil or vapour.

Not having a removable lid means that any new wires have to be fed in from the end. This becomes progressively more difficult as the number of wires involved increases, so conduit should always be bigger than is initially required to allow for later additions, and should include pull cords so that you can pull wiring through rather than trying to push it.

Tie bases and 'P' clips

Cable tie bases are attached to bulkheads etc by screws and provide a secure, single-point mounting to which a small number of wires can be secured with cable ties. Some bases can be used to secure round conduit or water pipes. 'P' clips are ideal for securing single cables as long as the clip grips the cable securely.

This haphazard mass of connections (above) are replaced with a new panel and rail-mounted terminals (below). Note the use of cable ties to tidy the wiring.

Connections

Good connections are essential in achieving a safe and reliable electrical system. Loose connections cause intermittent interruptions to the power supply to equipment, and get hot because of sparks or arcing at the connection itself. If high currents are involved, this heating effect can be enough to cause a fire.

'Chocolate block' connectors can only be recommended if they have a stainless steel barrier to eliminate contact of the screw with the cable strands. They are also subject to corrosion because of dissimilar metals, ie nickel-plated screws, brass bodies and copper strands. Although useful, they are the least desirable of connectors, DIN rail connectors are much more preferable and professional. (See the bottom photo on page 44)

Soldering

Soldering has to be carried out correctly if it is to provide a reliable connection, and achieving a good result is difficult on large joints. I prefer to leave soldered joints to the small connections – usually factory-made – associated with electronic equipment.

Crimping

Crimping offers a more reliable joint, but it too has to be done correctly, and using the proper tool.

Although many people use single jaw crimping tools because they are cheap, the correct crimping action on an insulated terminal involves two crimps – one where the wire's strands are located inside the terminal, and one where the wire's insulation is located inside the terminal's insulating sleeve. This second crimp helps to secure the wire to the terminal and allows the insulation to absorb vibration and movement. Double jaw tools can be used. They perform both crimping actions in one movement, and on some models the crimping pressure can be adjusted.

Crimped sleeves can be applied to wire ends to provide mechanical protection to wires that are to be connected to screw type terminals. The need for these, however, can be eliminated by using screw/clamp terminals.

Deck fittings

Deck plugs and sockets need regular maintenance on their contacts and terminals to eliminate corrosion. Through deck glands eliminate the electrical joints of plugs and sockets above deck, and the terminations can be made below deck, where they can be kept dry and easily accessible.

Over a period of time, the rubber inserts of compression glands and plugs can go hard and crack. To minimize this, cover the gland with a moulded sleeving or wrap it with self-amalgamating tape.

Where wiring comes out of holes in pushpit or pulpit railings for things such as navigation lights and aerials, the holes are usually drilled through from the outside leaving sharp burrs on the inside which will damage the wire. To eliminate this problem, PVC sleeving can be fitted over the wire and pushed into the hole leaving some of the sleeve outside and some inside.

Where cables enter or exits the mast they should be sleeved or fitted with rubber grommets to prevent chafing. Sleeving – such as split convolute tubing – fitted to the wiring outside the mast will help to protect it.

6 Monitoring

Monitoring a DC electrical system requires three types of instrument, a **voltmeter** (measuring volts), an **ammeter** (measuring amps), and an **amp-hour meter** measuring the amount of charge that has flowed into or out of the battery.

All three can be incorporated into a single unit – usually the amp-hour meter – but it is often useful to have the different instruments in different places. A voltmeter and ammeter, for instance, are often located with the engine instruments in the wheelhouse or cockpit area, but it is also handy to have a voltmeter in the navigation area, while the amp-hour meter is of more use on or near the distribution panel.

Voltmeter

On most production boats, a voltmeter is located on the engine panel and connected to the starting switch, to show the engine battery voltage when the engine is running. It may be more prudent, though, to have two voltmeters – one monitoring each bank of batteries and have these operated by the battery isolating switches. This means that any auxiliary charging systems that are fitted such as solar panels can be monitored even when the engine is switched off.

When installing a voltmeter, it is important to appreciate that the instrument has to be connected 'in parallel' to the battery: in other words, it has to be connected between the two battery terminals. It is particularly important, therefore, to include a fuse or circuit breaker to prevent it from short circuiting the battery if the meter develops a fault.

Ammeter

Ammeters can be divided into two main groups: 'centre zero' types, which can show both charge and discharge; and 'full scale' types

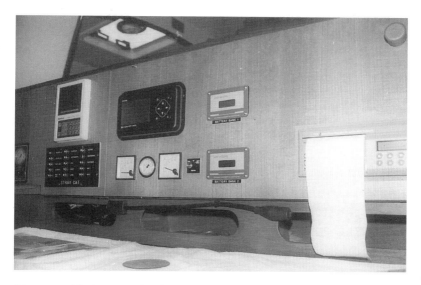

Above and below: navigation table panel layout on *Stray Cat* showing Loran receiver above circuit breaker panel, Philips GPS above voltmeter (left) and ammeter (right). The switch to the right of the ammeter selects either the output from the solar panels or the water powered alternator to be displayed on the ammeter. The amp-hour meters are shown for battery bank 1 and battery bank 2.

which can show charge or discharge, depending on how they are connected in the circuitry.

Unfortunately, because an ammeter measures current, it has to be placed 'in series' as part of the circuit it is monitoring. In the case of a charging circuit, for instance, this means that the output wiring from the alternator has to lead up to the ammeter and back down to the battery. Increasing the length of the charging circuit like this introduces voltage drops, and reduces its efficiency. A good alternative is to use what is known as a 'shunt ammeter'. It is more expensive, but is a more efficient way of monitoring current.

The shunt is a very low resistance that is placed in the circuit that is to be monitored. As current flows through the shunt, the resistance creates a voltage drop, so there is a difference in voltage between one end of the shunt and the other. This difference in voltage is directly proportional to the current flowing through the shunt. The shunt ammeter is, in fact, a voltmeter with a scale marked off in amps, that can be connected to the shunt by a pair of relatively thin wires.

Amp-hour meter

An amp-hour meter measures the overall performance of the electrical system and the amount of battery capacity available, so it is particularly useful to have one connected to the service battery.

An external shunt is used connected to the negative terminal of the battery. A connection is then made to the meter as well as a connection to the battery, usually the service batteries. The shunt monitors current going into the batteries (charge) and current going out of the batteries (discharge). The voltage connection measures battery terminal voltage (see Fig 6.1).

With practice, and manufacturers' guidance notes, you can work out exactly when to run the engine to charge the batteries, rather than just running the engine daily for a certain time and hoping that the batteries are charged. Normally the meter will show a resultant sum of the charge and discharge current, depending on the amount of consumption of the various loads and charge from the charging devices.

If more charge is going into the batteries than is being consumed then the amps will show a positive value. If, on the other hand, more amps are being consumed than being put into the batteries from the charging sources, the amps will show a negative value.

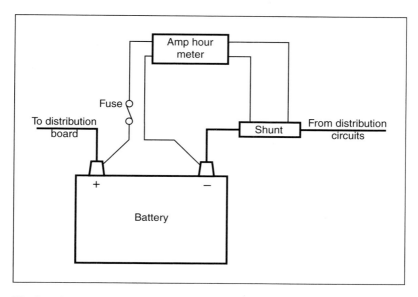

Fig 6.1 Amp-hour meter connections.

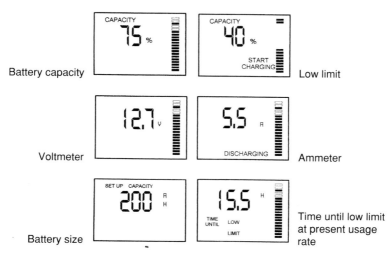

Fig 6.2 The MES Battery Management System includes an alternator controller and a meter which monitors volts, amps and amp hours and displays the values of the set-up settings that can be made to suit the charging system and the type of batteries.

The Link 10 amp-hour meter uses the same size mounting hole (51 mm/2 in) as most engine monitoring instruments. It displays volts, amps, amp hours, charge remaining and time remaining at present consumption. A multi-colour bar graph displays battery state of charge at a glance and the meter can also show a record of past information, including the deepest discharge, number of recharge cycles and average discharge.

7 On board equipment

The more energy efficient your on board equipment is, the less electrical energy it will use, so the less often you will need to charge your batteries. The items of equipment that drain the batteries most when cruising are:

- Lighting
- Refrigerator
- Autopilot
- Instruments

Lighting

Good quality light fittings are essential, and should be regularly checked for corrosion at their connections to the wiring and at the contact surfaces of the bulb. Any corrosion will create a voltage drop which will reduce the output from the light; this is particularly important for the navigation lights.

Cabin lighting should be divided into different circuits so that if a circuit breaker trips or a fuse blows in one circuit, others remain operative and some lighting is available.

Energy efficient lighting

DC lights that have single or double 8 watt fluorescent tubes are more energy efficient than filament bulbs with a greater light output. An 8 watt fluorescent fitting will draw 0.7 amps with the equivalent output of a 25 watt filament bulb.

Energy efficient compact fluorescent transistorized lights are available for use with low voltage DC, and are even more efficient:

Compact fluorescent lamp (watts)	Amps	Equivalent filament lamp (watts)
5	0.52	25
7	0.68	40
9	0.85	60
11	1.00	75

they cost a bit more than filament lamps, but can produce more than five times as much light for the same power consumption.

Halogen lights

For bright, concentrated lighting, halogen lamps are unbeatable. They are generally more expensive than filament lamps but produce more light per amp consumed. Their bright light makes them ideal for areas used for reading.

Swivelling bulkhead-mounted fittings are good for the saloon chart table and bunk areas, but halogen lights need to be installed with some care because they produce a lot of heat. If recessed fittings are used, the heat may be confined into a small space behind the fitting and cause heat damage to surrounding surfaces. It is important to follow the manufacturers' recommendations.

Halogen lights installed on spreaders or as part of the steaming light fitting are popular and produce a good illumination of the deck area.

A waterproof light fitted to the pulpit rail or mounted on the deck in such a way that the light illuminates the water ahead of the vessel is a useful accessory when hauling the anchor. Alternatively, a waterproof deck socket can be installed in the bow area and a hand-held light with wandering lead plugged into the socket allowing the light to be directed where needed.

General lighting

A mixture of compact fluorescent lights for overall illumination and halogen lamps for concentrated light in the areas where it is needed will result in an efficient lighting layout that will probably reduce the number of lights that have to be switched on to produce the desired effect.

Night lights

For blue water cruising, or passages involving night sailing, it is a good idea to include red night lights, especially in the companion-way area: this reduces glare in the cockpit area and lets the helmsman go below without having to wait for his eyes to adjust to the change in light level. A separate circuit for the night lights or a change-over system from ordinary to night lights is a useful addition which can be selected by the skipper or helmsman.

Refrigeration

Most boats are fitted with air-cooled refrigerators produced in large numbers for the caravan and motorhome market. The heat taken from the interior of the fridge to cool it has to be dissipated outside through a heat exchanger, usually in the form of a grid mounted on the back of the fridge. If this type of refrigerator is built into an enclosed space such as a galley unit, ventilation holes have to be provided to increase the flow of air around the heat exchanger. Unfortunately, this raises the temperature of the air inside the boat – which is probably not what you are trying to achieve in hot weather.

Water-cooled refrigerators

Water-cooled refrigeration units are more expensive but are generally much more efficient.

Installing a water-cooled unit may mean installing a custom-made cool box, but this too can be an advantage, as the insulation can be made very thick and thermally efficient. Alternatively do-it-yourself installation kits are available to fit into existing refrigerators using either holding plates or evaporators and water-cooled condensers/heat exchangers.

Holding plate refrigerators

In a holding plate system, the compressor operates at high speed to freeze the plate as quickly as possible while the engine is running or a mains-powered battery charger is operating. As soon as the engine is stopped or the charger switched off, the compressor stops.

The holding plate should stay cold for 8–20 hours, but if more cooling is required, the compressor starts up at low speed and for short periods to maintain the holding plate's temperature at a pre-set level thus minimizing battery drain.

Evaporator refrigerators

Like their commoner air-cooled counterparts, water-cooled refrigerators with evaporators are of the 'constant cycling' type which are switched on and off by a thermostat mounted inside. They are generally smaller than holding plate systems as only small amounts of cooling are required on a continuous basis.

The frequency of operation of either unit, and consequently the electrical demand, will depend on the size of the refrigerator, how

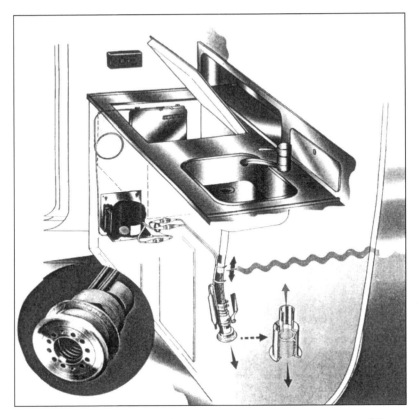

Fig 7.1 Isotherm self-pumping fridge operation. The Isotherm SP unit consists of three main components: the compressor, the through-hull fitting, and the evaporator/holding plate. The through-hull fitting replaces any other through-hull fitting (such as the galley sink drain) and contains the copper nickel heat exchanger. The refrigerant is piped to the fitting and the movement of the boat produces the self-pumping action which cools it.

well insulated it is and how efficient the cooling of the refrigerant is.

With standard water cooled systems the current used by the water pump, although small, has to be added to that of the compressor to give an accurate overall consumption, but other cooling methods can be used which incorporate water cooling without the need for a pumped water cooling system, such as the Isotherm SP, Fig 7.1 and Frigomatic K keel/heat exchanger, page 62. This not only reduces their power consumption, but also makes them smaller and quieter.

Insulation

When building a custom-made unit, it is important to allow space for plenty of insulation, because the better the quality and thickness of the insulation the less energy the fridge will consume.

Suitable locations for custom-built refrigerators are under seats in the saloon or under bunks. In either location, if there is space between the seat or bunk and the hull where the refrigerator is installed, it can be filled with expanding foam, thereby helping to support the unit, as well as providing extra insulation, providing maximum insulation and additional buoyancy for the boat.

Further information on installing custom-built refrigerators is available from the book *Heating and Cooling On Board* by E Lamprecht, published by Adlard Coles Nautical.

Using the engine to power equipment

If the engine has to be run to charge the batteries, then it makes sense to use its power for other purposes as well, such as to use the cooling water to heat a calorifier; effectively producing hot water from waste heat. The engine can also be used to make fresh water, run the refrigerator and charge the batteries at the same time. This makes economical use of the engine power and adds load to the engine which is good for a diesel. (See Case History 3.)

A refrigerator compressor can be run mechanically from the engine. This method is best suited to the holding plate method of refrigeration, but it does mean the engine must be run every day or more frequently if the ambient temperature is high.

If finances permit, you could even add a belt-driven water maker; but check with the engine manufacturers that it is suitable for this.

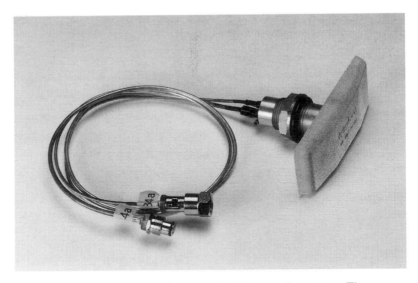

The hull-mounted heat exchanger of a Frigomatic system. The Frigomatic K unit eliminates the need for a water pump by using a keel cooler heat exchanger to cool the refrigerant. The compressor pumps the refrigerant to an exchanger mounted outside the hull. The heat exchanger is made from the same sintered bronze material used for ground/earth plates and so can be used as a ground plate for the electrical system as an additional bonus.

Autopilots and instruments

An autopilot can be a major consumer of electrical power, especially if it is in almost constant use. Even a modest average consumption of 5 amps adds up to 120 Ah over a 24 hour period, and the actual consumption can be considerably increased if the pilot is having to work hard.

The use of wind-powered generator, solar panels and water-powered generator, as supplementary charging systems, will help to maintain the batteries' charge level.

Windvane self-steering systems are an option that is non electrical. Windvanes cannot, therefore, usually be linked to electronic navigation instruments and waypoints plotted for the voyage.

Instrument power consumption

Instruments require power to operate and although their individual current drain may be small, the fact that they may be left on all the time makes them significant consumers.

Radar is often the most power-hungry piece of equipment used. In bad visibility it may be required to be on constantly but if it can be left in standby mode the power it consumes can be reduced to less than half on some models.

Sailing instruments will be needed continuously for wind, compass, depth, speed and navigation data. Many of these functions can be incorporated into one unit that can serve as repeaters at the navigation table. These will all consume a small amount of power individually but their total value must be taken into account, especially if backlighting is used which can triple the overall consumption and add to the amp hours demanded from the batteries. GPS units, chart plotters etc will all add to the total amp hours, so use of standby/sleep modes is an advantage, and again backlighting should be taken into account, and adjusted to as low a level as possible.

8 Case histories

Case history 1: *Flint*

Flint is a Moody 36 yacht owned since new by its present owner. Over the years *Flint*'s electrical system has been upgraded to cope with the additional power demands being made as new equipment is fitted.

The battery banks consist of two 105 Ah lead calcium batteries for the services, and one 105 Ah lead calcium battery for engine starting, with a rotary isolator switch to control starting and charging of the batteries.

Over the course of a weekend's sailing, the drain on the batteries is typically in the region of 40 to 50 amp hours, which would normally require the engine to be run for a couple of hours a day, so an Adverc BM alternator controller was fitted to uprate the alternator's output and keep the engine running time to a minimum.

Solar panel on *Flint*.

To provide additional charging, without the need to run the engine unnecessarily, a Siemens SP70 solar panel was installed on top of the cockpit cover roof. The output from the solar panel is up to 4 amps depending on conditions, so it provides enough continuous charge to supply the demand of the air-cooled refrigerator during the day – it was switched off at night.

The refrigerator is normally cooled before leaving the marina, when the battery charger is in use, and the shore power supply is connected. The battery charger is therefore doing two jobs: topping up the batteries and cooling the refrigerator.

A Rutland 913 wind-powered generator was later installed to provide additional charge to allow the refrigerator to be left on all night.

Overall, the addition of the solar panel and the wind generator means that in good conditions, enough charge is produced to meet all the boat's power demands without running the engine at all.

Rutland wind generator on *Flint.*

Case history 2: *Rival Spirit*

Rival Spirit is a 38 foot Rival, whose owners undertook an extensive refit before taking a year off work to sail from the south coast of England to South America, via the Madeira, Canary and Cape Verde Islands, returning via the Caribbean.

New lead calcium batteries were installed, and the engine alternator was replaced by a more powerful 55 amp unit with a Kestrel alternator controller.

The Kestrel was adjusted to limit the output to 40 amps continuous to reduce strain on the alternator, and prevent it overheating in the engine space, particularly in tropical climates. The maximum output of the alternator, with the Kestrel switched off, was 20 amps tapering down to 3 or 4.

The engine would need to be run every two days or so, for a couple of hours, to recharge the batteries and rapidly cool the refrigerator – determined by the amp-hour meter reading and experience.

To reduce the length of the cable runs, a shunt ammeter was fitted to the engine instrument panel with its shunt connected between the alternator output and the starter motor main terminal; the starter cables were used as part of the circuit back to the batteries.

A towed water-powered generator is deployed when cruising speeds reach 4 knots or more, and produces enough output for the navigation lights and instruments at normal cruising speeds.

During the day the navigation lights are off, but the water-cooled Isotherm ASU refrigerator (see Chapter 7) is on, as are the navigation instruments and autopilot, but two 55 watt Siemens solar panels supplement the charge from the towed alternator. Average battery consumption would be 2 amp hours during the daylight hours. The autopilot's consumption was an average of 4 amp hours' and night time cruising with navigation lights, instruments, occasional cabin lights, autopilot on and the refrigerator off would result in battery consumption of approximately 4 amp hours during the night.

The electrical system on *Rival Spirit* has proved reliable, and the batteries remained in good condition and charge throughout the voyage.

The additional charge from the towed alternator and solar panels reduced the need to run the engine for battery charging, allowed the refrigerator to remain in a cold state and to keep the navigation lights on all night.

Case history 3: *Stray Cat*

Stray Cat is a 37 foot Prout Snowgoose Elite catamaran that has been extensively refitted for round the world cruising.

Many leisure boat owners get by using conventional automotive lead acid batteries and charging methods, but long term cruising requires a radical rethink.

In this case, conventional lead acid batteries have been replaced with Saft's SRM nickel cadmium cells (see Chapter 2) divided into three banks. One bank consists of ten 1.2 volt, 80 amp hour cells, giving 12 volts and 80 amp hours capacity for engine starting; the other two banks each have ten 1.2 volt 220 amp hour cells giving 220 amp hours capacity for each bank (see page 12).

The reliability of the nickel cadmium technology is an important factor on a yacht intended to cross oceans and operate in extreme climates.

The sintered/plastic bonded technology of the cells means the voltage of the battery banks is similar to lead acid batteries, so conventional charging methods can be employed without adjustments required.

Stray Cat has several charging methods available:

• Engine-driven alternator
• Three 55 watt solar panels
• A water-driven alternator
• A wind generator
• A combined mains-powered battery charger (50 amps)/inverter (1500 watts at 230 volts AC)

Two changeover switches are used for the battery switching allowing all, two, or one bank to be connected to the electrical distribution or charging systems, providing a variety of options for charging and distribution as can be seen in the original system, Fig 8.1, and the uprated system, Fig 8.2.

The main alternator has a Kestrel alternator controller fitted which boosts its output and converts it to a battery sensing and constant current unit (see Chapter 4). Charging by this method is therefore achieved in a shorter space of time which reduces the engine run time and saves fuel.

The three Siemens 55 watt solar panels are fitted on top of the custom-made cockpit cover. While all the fitting out work was being done on *Stray Cat*, a charge of 9 amps was recorded from the solar panels at lunch time, one day in May at Canvey Island, England, and the panels have proved even more efficient in more tropical

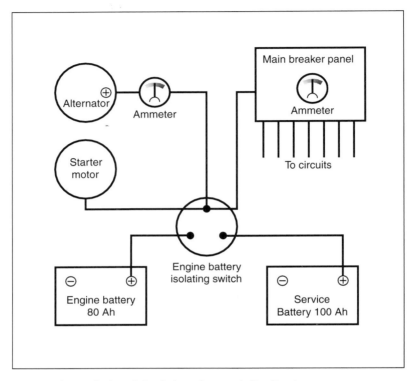

Fig 8.1 *Stray Cat*'s original charging and distribution system.

regions, where they are able to produce about 70 amp hours per day on average.

The water-driven alternator (see page 38) is powered by a turbine towed behind *Stray Cat*, in much the same way as a trailing log, and generates about 4.5 amp hours of charge at normal cruising speed, or the alternator part of the generator can be detached, wind vanes attached, and then hoisted up the halyards to become a wind-powered generator, when at anchor or in a marina.

The water-driven alternator will provide the most charge as it will be generating for 24 hours when cruising (about 108 amp hours) whereas the solar panels will be producing charge for about 10 hours a day.

The estimated electrical consumption per day is 180 amp hours to run the lights, instruments, radar, SSB radio, audio system, inverter for 230 volt AC supply, refrigerator, cabin fans etc.

While under way, the solar panels produce about 70 Ah per day

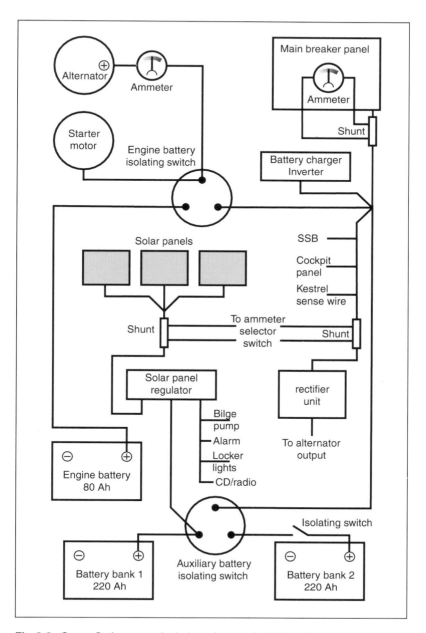

Fig 8.2 *Stray Cat*'s upgraded charging and distribution system.

and the Aquair unit produces about 108 Ah per day, so together they should provide just enough charge to meet the demand, but energy efficient equipment is essential to minimize the demand, as is the need to conserve energy by eliminating unnecessary waste and switching off lights and equipment when not needed.

The refrigeration on *Stray Cat* is custom built using a water-cooled Frigoboat unit whose evaporator plate is placed inside a pur-pose-built compartment located under the starboard aft berth. The water-cooled compressor is located at the bottom of the hanging locker and operates, on average, for about five minutes every hour, when the thermostat is set at +3° C, an ideal temperature for keep-ing drinking water, salads etc cool. Total current consumption of the compressor and cooling pump is about 4 amps, so when it is running for five minutes per hour its average consumption is 0.3 amp hours. The unit can also be set to operate as a freezer, with cold air from the freezer compartment being used to cool the neigh-bouring compartment which then becomes a refrigerator.

Using the on board microwave oven, through a DC to AC inverter (Victron Combi 12/1500), does not consume much battery capacity. For example, if the current demanded by the inverter, to power the microwave, is 100 amps and the microwave is only on for five min-utes, the amp hours consumed would be 100 amps $\times$ $1/12$ hour, or 8.33 amp hours.

Although the engine is primarily for manoeuvring, there are other ways to make use of its power. Attached to *Stray Cat*'s engine is a belt-driven water maker, which can produce 20 litres fresh water an hour from salt water or 15 litres an hour from clean river water. The lower figure for fresh water produced from river water is due to the larger particles of silt present, compared to the much smaller particles of salt in sea water.

Another function is to heat the hot water cylinder using the engine-cooling water, so clothes washing etc can be done at the same time, and while the engine is running, battery charging is an additional bonus, supplementing the solar panels.

The engine therefore performs three important tasks as well as manoeuvring *Stray Cat*. This is particularly useful when at anchor. In September 1996 the owners spent four weeks at anchor off Villa Real de Santo Antonio at the mouth of the Rio Guadiana in Southern Portugal, without the need to go into a marina for fresh water or to charge the batteries. The engine was run only to replen-ish the water tanks, during this period, and this was required to be done every couple of days for a period of approximately three hours.

All this electrical efficiency requires monitoring to ensure that it stays efficient. *Stray Cat*'s monitoring system is designed for this and is user-friendly. There are two voltmeters monitoring the aux-iliary services, one is fitted to the main circuit breaker panel, and the other to the navigation panel above the chart table. Also located on the navigation panel are two amp-hour meters which monitor the two auxiliary battery banks. These register zero when the bat-teries are fully charged and progressively read negative as the bat-teries are being used. A certain reading tells you when to recharge the batteries.

As various elements of the overall charging system are operating all the time – wind, solar, turbine, battery charger or engine alter-nator – the amp hour meters should, in theory, never reach the level where the batteries are in a discharged state. In normal use, the amp hour meters should show a very slow rate of discharge, or charge, depending on the amount of consumption and the amount of charging available. The navigation panel also has an ammeter which can display the charging current being produced by either the solar panels or the water powered alternator – via a changeover switch.

The key to this electrical system design is flexibility. There are many loads, many power sources, and three battery banks. The sys-tem must also be reliable.

Electrical system design is often not a high priority of owners of small craft, but an uprated system can greatly add to the enjoy-ment of cruising.

Glossary of Terms

Ampere (amp) The SI unit of electric current, approximately equivalent to the flow of 6×10^{18} electrons per second. Named after AM Ampere (1775–1836).

Amp hour The practical unit of quantity of electricity. One amp of current flowing for one hour is one amp hour.

Ampere hour capacity The term used to describe the capacity of a battery.

Auto wiring cable This is used in the automobile industry. It is PVC insulated cable with a wide selection of colours. Available from 0.5mm^2 to 60mm^2.

AWG American Wire Gauge, the term used by the USA for the size of the conducting cores of a cable.

Cable tray A cable support consisting of a continuous base with raised edges and no covering. A cable tray has more than 30% of material removed from the base to form slots.

Cable trunking A manufactured enclosure for the protection of cables, normally of rectangular cross section, of which one side is removable or hinged.

Circuit breaker A device capable of making, carrying and breaking normal load currents and also making and automatically breaking, under pre-determined conditions, abnormal currents such as short-circuit currents and overload currents.

Conduit A part of a closed wiring system for cables in electrical installations, allowing them to be drawn in and/or replaced, but not inserted laterally.

Current carrying capacity The maximum current which can be carried by a conductor under specified conditions without its steady state temperature exceeding a specified value.

Electric current An electric current is said to flow through a conductor when there is an overall movement of electric charge through it. The unit of electric current is the ampere.

Electric circuit The complete path traversed by an electric current.

Flame retardant A 'flame-retardant' material is one which, having been ignited, does not continue to burn, or burns for a very limited period, after the source of heat has been removed.

Fuse A device that, by the fusing of its element, opens the circuit in which it is inserted by breaking the current when this exceeds a given value for a sufficient time.

Gel battery A lead-plated battery that has its electrolyte in a gel form and not liquid.

Lead acid battery Lead-plated battery that has its electrolyte as a dilute sulphuric acid liquid.

Nickel cadmium battery (Nicad) Nickel and cadmium plated batteries with an alkaline electrolyte.

Ohm The derived SI unit of resistance defined as the resistance between two points of a conductor when a constant difference of potential of one volt, applied between these two points, produces in the conductor a current of one ampere. Named after Georg Ohm (1787–1854).

Tri-rated cable Rated for use in UK/USA/Canada (BS/UL/CSA), hence the term tri-rated. PVC insulated cable with temperature rating of 95/105°C; available from 0.5mm^2 to 300mm^2.

Volt The derived SI unit of electrical potential defined as the difference of potential between two points on a conducting wire carrying a constant current of one ampere when the power dissipated between these points is one watt. Named after Alessandro Volta (1745–1827).

Watt The derived SI unit of power, equal to one joule per second. The energy expended per second by an unvarying electric current of one ampere flowing through a conductor the ends of which are maintained at a potential difference of one volt. Named after James Watt (1736–1819).

Welding cable Heat resistant, oil resistant and flame retardant (HOFR) cable, very flexible with temperature rating of 85°C. Available from 16mm^2 to 240mm^2.

Appendix 1

Amp hour consumption table

Equipment	Watts	@ 12v =	Amps	x hrs/day	= Amp hours
autopilot	25.00		2.10	6.00	12.60
nav. instruments	12.00		1.00	24.00	24.00
nav. lamps	30.00		2.50	10.00	25.00
VHF reception	6.00		0.50	5.00	2.50
VHF transmission	60.00		5.00	0.10	0.50
radar (active)	36.00		3.00	1.00	3.00
radar (standby)	10.00		0.83	12.00	9.96
'fridge (air cooled)	50.00		4.50	8.00	36.00
water pump	30.00		2.50	0.30	0.75
radio/cassette	30.00		2.50	8.00	20.00
cabin/night lights	25.00		2.10	4.00	8.40
instrument lamps	2.00		0.16	10.00	1.60
compass light	2.00		0.16	10.00	1.60
sundry use	30.00		2.50	3.00	7.50
Total					**153.41**

This table gives typical amp hour consumption for a 12 volt system over a 24 hour period on a cruising yacht. With a daily requirement of 154 amp hours, the battery amp hour capacity required will be:

$154 \times 2.0 = 308$ amp hours for lead acid
$154 \times 1.3 = 200$ amp hours for gel
$154 \times 1.0 = 154$ amp hours for nickel cadmium

Appendix 2   Cable size table

The table opposite gives the cable size required, in mm², for a given circuit length in metres, and the maximum continuous current permissible in the circuit, for a volt drop of 1 volt at the load terminals using the given cable size. The calculations to obtain the cable size are based on the resistivity of copper at 50°C. To determine the maximum current in a cable, derating correction factors for expected ambient temperature and bundling should be included. The value of the current should be multiplied by the correction factors to determine the derated value of the current in the cable.

Correction factors for ambient temperature							
Ambient temperature	25°C	30°C	35°C	40°C	50°C	60°C	70°C
General purpose PVC 60/70°C	1.03	1.0	0.94	0.82	0.58	0.5	0.35
Heat resisting PVC 85°C	1.02	1.0	0.95	0.9	0.8	0.83	0.47
Tri-rated PVC to BS/UL/CSA standards 95/105°C	1.14	1.09	1.05	1.0	0.9	0.77	0.71

Bundling correction factor

If more than six cables are bundled together, ie seven or more single core cables or more than three two core cables, a correction factor of 0.8 should be used.

Cable sizes (mm²) for 1.0 volt drop in 12 volt systems (2.0 volts for 24 volt systems)

length \ amps	1	2	3	4	5	7.5	10	12.5	15	17.5	20	25	30	35	40	50	60	70	80	90	100
3	0.75	0.75	0.75	0.75	0.75	0.75	1.0	1.0	1.5	1.5	1.5	2.5	2.5	4.0	4.0	4.0	6.0	6.0	6.0	10.0	10.0
4	0.75	0.75	0.75	0.75	0.75	0.75	1.0	1.5	1.5	1.5	2.5	2.5	4.0	4.0	4.0	6.0	6.0	6.0	10.0	10.0	10.0
5	0.75	0.75	0.75	0.75	0.75	1.0	1.5	1.5	2.5	2.5	2.5	4.0	4.0	4.0	6.0	6.0	10.0	10.0	10.0	10.0	16.0
6	0.75	0.75	0.75	0.75	0.75	1.0	1.5	2.5	2.5	2.5	4.0	4.0	4.0	6.0	6.0	10.0	10.0	10.0	16.0	16.0	16.0
7	0.75	0.75	0.75	0.75	0.75	1.5	1.5	2.5	2.5	4.0	4.0	4.0	6.0	6.0	6.0	10.0	10.0	16.0	16.0	16.0	16.0
8	0.75	0.75	0.75	0.75	1.0	1.5	2.5	2.5	4.0	4.0	4.0	6.0	6.0	6.0	10.0	10.0	16.0	16.0	16.0	16.0	25.0
9	0.75	0.75	0.75	0.75	1.0	1.5	2.5	2.5	4.0	4.0	4.0	6.0	6.0	10.0	10.0	10.0	16.0	16.0	16.0	25.0	25.0
10	0.75	0.75	0.75	1.0	1.5	2.5	2.5	4.0	4.0	4.0	6.0	6.0	10.0	10.0	10.0	16.0	16.0	16.0	25.0	25.0	25.0
12	0.75	0.75	1.0	1.0	1.5	2.5	4.0	4.0	4.0	6.0	6.0	10.0	10.0	10.0	16.0	16.0	16.0	25.0	25.0	25.0	35.0
14	0.75	0.75	1.0	1.5	1.5	2.5	4.0	4.0	6.0	6.0	6.0	10.0	10.0	16.0	16.0	16.0	25.0	25.0	25.0	35.0	35.0
16	0.75	0.75	1.5	1.5	2.5	4.0	4.0	6.0	6.0	6.0	10.0	10.0	16.0	16.0	16.0	25.0	25.0	25.0	35.0	35.0	35.0
18	0.75	1.0	1.5	2.5	2.5	4.0	4.0	6.0	6.0	10.0	10.0	10.0	16.0	16.0	16.0	25.0	25.0	35.0	35.0	35.0	50.0
20	0.75	1.0	1.5	2.5	2.5	4.0	6.0	6.0	10.0	10.0	10.0	16.0	16.0	16.0	25.0	25.0	35.0	35.0	35.0	50.0	50.0
25	0.75	1.5	2.5	2.5	4.0	4.0	6.0	10.0	10.0	10.0	16.0	16.0	16.0	25.0	25.0	35.0	35.0	50.0	50.0	50.0	70.0
30	0.75	1.5	2.5	4.0	4.0	6.0	10.0	10.0	10.0	16.0	16.0	16.0	25.0	25.0	35.0	35.0	50.0	50.0	70.0	70.0	70.0
35	0.75	1.5	2.5	4.0	4.0	6.0	10.0	10.0	16.0	16.0	16.0	25.0	25.0	35.0	35.0	50.0	50.0	70.0	70.0	70.0	95.0
40	1.0	2.5	4.0	4.0	4.0	6.0	10.0	16.0	16.0	16.0	25.0	25.0	35.0	35.0	35.0	50.0	70.0	70.0	70.0	95.0	95.0
50	1.5	2.5	4.0	6.0	6.0	10.0	16.0	16.0	16.0	25.0	25.0	35.0	35.0	50.0	50.0	70.0	70.0	95.0	95.0	120.0	120.0

Appendix 3   Equipment manufacturers' addresses

Batteries

Lead calcium plate batteries
Delphi EEMS, PO Box 336, Blackfriars House, 399 South Row,
Witan Gate, Central Milton Keynes, Buckinghamshire,
MK9 2DT, UK
Fax + 44 (0) 1908 352217

Sonnenschein gel batteries
CMP Batteries, 14 Gunnels Wood Park, Stevenage,
Hertfordshire, SG1 2BH, UK
Tel +44 (0) 1438 359090   *Fax* +44 (0) 1438 727684
E-mail cmp.standby@binternet.com

Exide Corporation, PO Box 14250, 645 Penn Street, Reading,
Pennsylvania, USA
Tel +1 610 378 0500   *Fax* +1 610 371 0462

Nickel cadmium batteries
Saft Nife Ltd, Pereguin Road, Hainault, Ilford,
Essex, IG6 3XJ, UK
Tel +44 (0) 181 498 1183   *Fax* +44 (0) 181 498 1113
E-mail sales@saft.alcatel-alsthom.co.uk
www.saft.alcatel.com

Saft America Inc., Industrial Battery Division, 711 Industrial
Boulevard, PO Box 1886, Valdosta, Georgia 31601 USA.
Tel +1 912 247 2331   *Fax* +1 912 247 8486

Battery connections

Battery connection terminals are readily available from marine
factors and auto electrical factors.

Connection blocks and bus bars
Merlin Equipment, Unit 1, Hithercroft Court, Lupton Road,
Wallingford, Oxfordshire, OX10 9BT, UK
Tel +44 (0) 1491 824333   *Fax* +44 (0) 1491 824466

Blue Sea Systems, 3924-D Irongate Road, Bellingham,
Washington, WA98226 USA
Tel +1 360 738 8230   *Fax* +1 360 734 4195
E-mail conduct@bluesea.com
www.bluesea.com/electric/

Charging equipment

MES Battery Controller
MES Ltd, PO Box 3009, Littlehampton, West Sussex,
BN17 5SJ, UK
Tel +44 (0) 1903 714028   *Fax* +44 (0) 1903 713777

Heart Interface incharge regulator
Heart Interface Corporation, 21440 68th Avenue South, Kent,
WA 98032 USA
Tel +1 (253) 872 7225   *Fax* +1 (253) 872 3412
www.heartinterface.com

Merlin Equipment (as above)

Kestrel alternator controller
Acorn Engineering, 5 Turner Street, Denton, Manchester,
M34 3EG, UK
Tel +44 (0) 161 320 8023   *Fax* +44 (0) 161 320 4039

Adverc Battery Management
Adverc BM Ltd, 245 Trysull Road, Merry Hill, Wolverhampton,
West Midlands, WV3 7LG, UK
Tel +44 (0) 1902 380494   *Fax* +44 (0) 1902 380435
E-mail technicalsales@adverc.demon.co.uk
www.adverc.demon.co.uk

Marine Diesel Engineering, 4102 Alla Road, Los Angeles,
California, 9066 USA
Tel +1 (310) 301 9011   *Fax* +1 (310) 321 1981

Heart Interface Freedom chargers
See Heart Interface details above

Victron Titan chargers
IMV Victron (UK) Ltd, Wheatfield Way, Hinckley Fields,
Hinckley, Leicester, Leicestershire, LE1O lYG, UK
Tel +44 (0) 1455 618666   *Fax* +44 (0) 1455 611446
E-mail sales@imv.co.uk
www.victronenergie.nl

Siemens Solar Panels
Siemens Solar Technical Services and Systems, Siemens House,
Windmill Road, Sunbury on Thames, TW16 7HS, UK
Tel +44 (0) 1932 792846   *Fax* +44 (0) 1932 792973

Siemens Solar Industries, 4650 Adhor Lane, PO Box 6032,
Camarillo, California, CA 93011 USA
Tel +1 (805) 482 6800   *Fax* +1 (805) 388 6395
E-mail sunpower@solarpv.com
www.solarpv.com

Wind-powered generators
Marlec Engineering Co Ltd, Rutland House, Trevithick Road,
Corby, Northamptonshire, NN17 5XY, UK
Tel +44 (0) 1536 201588   *Fax* +44 (0) 1536 400211
E-mail marlec@dial.pipex.com
www.dialspace.dial.pipex.com/marlec

Water-powered generators
Aquair water-powered generator
Ampair (Lumic) Ltd, PO Box 416, Poole, Dorset,
BH12 3LZ, UK
Tel +44 (0) 1202 749994   *Fax* +44 (0) 1202 736653
E-mail ampair@ampair.com
www.ampair.com

Jack Rabbit Marine, 425 Fairfield Avenue, Building 4,
Stamford, Connecticut, CT 06902 USA
Tel +1 203 961 8133   *Fax* +1 203 961 0382
E-mail jackrabbitmarine@compuserve.com

Distribution equipment

Battery switches

Merlin Equipment (as above)
Blue Sea (as above)

Monitoring equipment

MES Battery Management System (as above)
Heart Interface Link 10 (as above)

Lighting, refrigeration and instruments

Energy efficient lighting
Stengel, Rembrandtstrasse 2, D-47877 Willich-Schiefbahn,
Germany
Tel +49 21 54 911575   *Fax* +49 21 54 911573
www.stengel.de

Marlec Engineering (as p 80)

Isotherm refrigeration
E-mail info@isotherm.com
www.isotherm.com

Sowester Marine Ltd, Stinsford Road, Nuffield, Poole, Dorset,
BH17 7SW, UK
Tel +44 (0) 1202 667700   *Fax* +44 (0) 1202 660888
E-mail kevin@sowester.co.uk
www.sowester.co.uk

Great Water Inc. 5148 Peach Street, Erie, Pennsylvania,
16509, USA
Tel +1 814 838 0796   *Fax* +1 814 838 8700
E-mail greatwater@csi.com
www.great-water.com

Frigomatic refrigeration
E-mail veco@uli.it
www.veco.net
Penguin Engineering Ltd, Furniss Way, Station Road,
Hayling Island, Hampshire, PO11 OED, UK
Tel +44 (0) 1705 465607   *Fax* +44 (0) 1705 461325

Simpson Lawrence USA Inc., 6208 28th Street East,
Bradenton, Florida, 34203-4488, USA
Tel +1 941 753 7533   *Fax* +1 941 746 7166

Index

Adverc Battery Management
   unit 31
Adverc BM alternator controller
   64
alternators 27–31
alternator controllers 28
American wire gauge (AWG)
   73
American wire gauge and metric
   conversion chart 21
ammeter 52–4
ampere 73
amp hour 73
amp-hour consumption table
   75
amp-hour meter 54–6
Ampair Aquair water-powered
   generator 38
amp-hour comparison chart
   12
auto wiring cable 21
autopilots 62–3

batteries 1–15
   bank size 5
   circuits 3
   engine start 5–6
   gel 9–10, 14, 74
   lead acid 5–8
   low maintenance 6
   nicad 10–12, 14, 74
   traction 6
battery banks 64
battery chargers 32–6
battery connections 16–21
battery terminals 16–18
battery wiring 20–1
boost charge 25
bus bars 19, 20

cables 45
cable size tables 76
cable trays 46, 48, 73

cable trunking 73
charging 22–39
charging equipment 27
circuit breakers 41, 42–3, 73
clamp connections 18
conduit 45–6, 48, 73
connection blocks 19, 20, 50
constant current charging 26
constant current regulators
   30
corrosion, protecting against
   18–19
crimping 50
current carrying capacity 73

deck fittings 51
Delco Voyager lead calcium
   plated batteries 8
distribution 40–51

energy efficient lighting 57–8
engine-driven alternator 67
engine start batteries 5–6
engine starting circuits 43
engine, using to power equipment
   61
equalize charge 25
evaporator refrigerator 59–60

float charge 25
fluorescent lamps 57
Frigomatic K unit 62
fuses 42–3, 73

gel batteries 9–10, 14, 74
generators 37–9

halogen lights 58
Heart Interface Freedom charger
   35
Heart Interface incharge
   regulator 30
holding plate refrigerators 59

isotherm ASU refrigerator 66
isotherm self-pumping fridge
  operation 60
instrument power consumption
  63
instruments 62–3
insulation 61
isolating switches 40, 41–2

Kestrel alternator controller 30,
  66
key switches 41

lead acid battery 14, 74
lead antimony plated batteries
  7
lead calcium plated batteries 7
lighting 57–8
Link 10 amp-hour meter 56
low maintenance batteries 6

mains-powered battery chargers
  32–6
maintenance-free batteries 6
MES battery management
  system 55
MES control/display head 28
monitoring a DC system 52–6

nickel cadmium (Nicad) batteries
  10–12, 14, 74
night lights 58

ohm 74
on board equipment 57–63

'p' clips 48
panels 43–5
pulse charging 26
pulse current regulators 31

refrigeration 59–61, 65
rotary switches 40
Rutland wind generator 65

Saft's SRM nicad cells 67
screw terminals 17–18
semi-traction batteries 6
slotted trunking 46–8
solar panels 36, 64, 66
solder type battery connections
  16
soldering 50

taper charging 22–4
threaded stud terminals 16–17
three-stage charging 24–6
three-stage graph 25
three-stage regulators 29
tie bases 48
towed alternator 66
traction batteries 6
tri-rated cable 21, 74
trunking 45–6, 48

Victron Energie Titan chargers
  32
Victron Pallas charger 33
volt 74
voltmeter 52

water-cooled refrigerators 59
water-driven alternator 67
water-powered generator 37–9,
  66
water tank analogy 13–15
watt 74
welding cable 21, 74
wind-powered generators 37,
  67
wiring 16–21